The ULTIMATE ASSIST

"The tremendous knowledge and sage wisdom Gr
is worth the price of admission. In *The Ultimate As*
only passes along his learnings from a life spent as
on every level, but also humbly offers his succe
in parenting his two daughters, who played at

MICHAEL JORDAN
NBA Hall-of-Famer

"Greg Nared has written a highly re
raise kids in an era where sports ar
lives. It is a value to all parents."

PHIL K
Co-Founder & Chair

"The Ultimate Assist is
to become high-level p
in our children that
the skill and will to
if they miss."

CEO, Dallas Maveric

The ULTIMATE
ASSIST

The ULTIMATE ASSIST

HELPING OUR KIDS SUCCEED
IN SPORTS & LIFE

GREG NARED

I dedicate this book to my wonderful daughters, Jacklin and Jaime.

Thank you for your ongoing support in all that I do. You, more than anyone else,

are the reason I had the ability to write this book.

CONTENTS

INTRODUCTION

PARENTING ATHLETES

With a few seconds left on the clock, my eldest daughter, Jackie, advanced the ball up the left side of the floor. My heart was pounding, my stomach in my throat. St Mary's was down two. I felt the nervous energy building in McKeon Pavilion, even through the pixelated online stream that brought me the game. With each dribble of the ball, the crowd grew more uneasy. I leaned forward in my seat.

The Lady Gaels were off to a hot start this season, 10-1, and this was the first conference game of the year. They took on West Coast Conference powerhouse Gonzaga, coached by the now-legendary Kelly Graves. The Zags were the nine-time defending WCC champs and ranked 24th in the nation for NCAA Division I Women's Basketball. In this game, St Mary's had more than held their own and so had Jackie. As usual, she led her team in scoring and everyone in the gym knew who was taking the final shot. One last chance to slay Goliath.

The Gonzaga defender met her just above the three-point line. Jackie stepped back, calculating her move. Sliding over to her spot on the right wing, her teammate positioned herself to screen the tenacious defender. I stood.

"Now's the time, Jackie!" I exclaimed for no one to hear. There were only three seconds on the clock. Crossing over, she made her move as her defender played her tight, fighting over the screen.

Two seconds.

Stopping on a dime at the top of the key, Jackie's quick pump fake sent the defender sailing by as she set her feet underneath her.

One second.

She released a three-pointer. Jackie and I had spent countless hours over the course of her life practicing this very shot: a straight-on three-pointer with a hand in her face. Feet set, elbow in, flick the wrist, let it fly. The ball hung in the air, sucking the oxygen from my lungs. It was like a small smooth stone hurling towards the forehead of a giant.

Swish!

The home crowd erupted as Jackie's teammates nearly tackled her. I screamed at my computer screen, hands in the air, "Let's go, Jackie!" I felt such tremendous pride in my daughter. Not just for the incredible moment she had just experienced, but also for the moments that brought her there. The work she put in: the early mornings and late nights, the hundreds of thousands of shots she had put up when no one was watching, the painstaking hours she spent studying the game. I was proud that she was living her dream. That she had worked to develop the character, discipline, and perseverance it takes to be the best on the court. I was, and still am, proud of the woman she has become.

If you are reading this book, I can only assume that you are a parent of an athlete yourself. If so, you likely have stories like mine, ones that make you extraordinarily proud of the child you are raising. Maybe they haven't yet reached the level Jackie had, but they remind you all the same of how blessed you are to see them push, struggle, and ultimately triumph. We, as parents, get a front-row seat to our kids' growth and development in sports and in life. And I want to help you make the most of it. That is really the heart of this book. To encourage and direct you as you navigate the crazy world of youth sports with your kids.

A big part of my job with the NBA's Dallas Mavericks is overseeing the strategic direction of our youth sports initiatives. I love it! Being around young people brings a spark to my heart and a smile to my face. I truly believe one of my gifts in life is to help young athletes reach their full potential on and off the court. When at a camp or tournament site, I high five every young athlete I pass and work hard to be available to give guidance and encouragement when necessary—to both athletes and parents. Young people are just plain fun, and I am thrilled to play a small part in their development.

That being said, youth sports is a unique and, at times, crazy world. I get asked by parents of athletes at least once a month, *What should I be doing to help my kid? How can I help them get the most out of their youth sports experience?* It is tough to know how to navigate the youth sports experience with your kids, especially considering how much it has changed over the years. These are not the same city recreation programs that you or I grew up with. These days, youth sports is a multibillion-dollar industry. It raked in an estimated

$19.2 billion in 2019 in the United States alone.[1] The average young athlete will spend over ten to twelve hours of their week[2] pursuing athletic endeavors and parents can spend thousands of dollars[3] a year on their children's athletic "careers."

My heart goes out to you as parents and to the young people you are raising. I remember what it was like to be an Uber driver, coach, chef, mental coach, personal trainer, number-one fan, and ATM, all while trying to balance the rest of my life. I've been in your shoes and I know what it is like to feel out of your league when it comes to your child's athletic journey. I admit I was somewhat caught off guard when my eldest first stepped into serious athletic competition, and I myself had to seek the advice of those who had been there before me.

My name is Greg Nared. I grew up a sports lover and competed at a high level. I had a verbal commitment to play quarterback for Ohio State, but instead opted to follow my passion by playing basketball for the University of Maryland. I have spent over thirty years working in the sports industry as an athlete business manager, agent, coach, and now the senior vice president for the Dallas Mavericks.

---

1 Christina Gough, "Youth Sports Market Size in the U.S. 2019," Statista, March 1, 2021, https://www.statista.com/statistics/1105433/youth-sports-market-size-usa/#:~:text=The%20youth%20sports%20market%20is,billion%20U.S.%20dollars%20by%202019.

2 "Survey: Kids Quit Most Sports By Age 11," AspenProjectPlay.org, The Aspen Institute Project Play, July 13, 2020, https://www.aspenprojectplay.org/national-youth-sport-survey/kids-quit-most-sports-by-age-11#:~:text=Among%20kids%20who%20do%20play,)%20%E2%80%93%20all%20around%20that%20mark.

3 "Youth Sports Facts: Challenges," AspenProjectPlay.org, The Aspen Institute Project Play, accessed March 24, 2021, https://www.aspenprojectplay.org/youth-sports-facts/challenges.

At my core, though, I am a parent just like you. I have simply been blessed to have connected with countless elite athletes in my lifetime and to build friendships with some all-time greats from every corner of the professional sports pantheon. In the process, I have learned a lot about raising athletes and the unique challenges their parents face.

On top of all that, I have had the honor of raising two daughters, Jackie and Jaime, who have both surpassed my own athletic achievements—and I am going to brag on my kids for a minute, if you don't mind.

Jackie holds the single season scoring record at SMC, has played professionally in Europe, and now coaches Division I NCAA Basketball at the University of Oregon. My younger daughter, Jaime, played basketball for the University of Tennessee, was drafted 13th overall in the WNBA draft to the Las Vegas Aces, and is currently playing professionally overseas.

I am pretty proud of them, if you couldn't tell.

I myself found sports at a young age, and it has without a doubt changed my life. It has taken me around the world, introduced me to amazing people, and given me incredible experiences. To this day, it continues to teach me about life, joy, and finding purpose. It has blessed my daughters beyond measure and connected us in a way I cannot express.

The game has been good to me.

And I am a firm believer that we are blessed in order to be a blessing to others. This is why I see it as my responsibility—and great joy—to give back to families who have the same vision my daughters and I have had: to use the amazing gift of sports as a catalyst for growth, development, and joy in our lives.

And it is not just my family that has benefitted. The U.S. Department of Education found, "High school athletes at the elite and varsity levels are more likely than nonathletes to have any postsecondary education by [eight years post high-school graduation] and to have earned a bachelor's degree by [eight years post high-school graduation]."[4] According to a study by Gallup, the majority of former collegiate students athletes are thriving in *five areas of well-being* that the study identified.[5] espnW in conjunction with EY Women Athletes Business Network surveyed four hundred female executives on four different continents and found that 94% of them played a sport growing up, with 61% of the respondents citing their sports involvement as a contributing factor to their success.[6]

It is clear that sports participation holds a huge benefit for those involved. Over the years, using my unique experience and resources, I have been able to help many young athletes develop and achieve their goals both in and outside the lines. Helping young people develop is in my DNA. I have seen firsthand the benefits that youth sports can have on a young person and how playing

---

4 Deven Carlson et al., "Nces.ed.gov," nces.ed.gov, National Center for Educational Statistics, U.S. Department of Education Institute of Education Sciences, September 2005, https://nces.ed.gov/pubs2005/2005303.pdf.

5 Brandon Busteed and Julie Ray, "Former Student-Athletes Are Winners in Well-Being," Gallup.com, Gallup, February 17, 2016, https://news.gallup.com/poll/189206/former-student-athletes-winners.aspx.

6 "Study: Women + Sports = Executive Success," ESPN-W, ESPN Internet Ventures, EY Women Athletes Network, October 9, 2014, https://www.espn.com/espnw/w-in-action/story/_/id/11669072/women-+-sports-=-executive-success.

sports can set them up for success in their future. Unfortunately, I know that I am limited in who I can help—primarily by time and space.

This is why I have written this book: to share what I have learned with a broader audience. To help families that I may never meet and guide, athletes I may never coach.

The focus of this book is twofold:

1. It will provide you with a practical pathway to raising a successful athlete who is also a healthy, successful, and socially responsible individual.

2. I hope what you find here helps you feel encouraged and supported as you raise daughters and sons who will have an experience that few are fortunate enough to have.

They do not write many books on this sort of thing—indeed, mine is the only one I am aware of—and parenting is hard enough, even without all the complexities of youth sports. My goal is that you are equipped to guide and direct your child as they put in the work in order to see the desired results.

I have designed this book to help you take an intentional and systematic approach to supporting your child's sports journey. In the process, you will enable them to gain the character and skills that will be a help to them for a lifetime.

Each chapter, I will be your guide, helping you to unpack key elements of parenting athletes as your child grows and develops. Before we dive into this journey together, I have a few quick thoughts.

First, though I recommend reading this book all the way through at least once, I also recommend coming back to it as your child grows and develops. It is impossible to implement everything you will find in this book all at once. Take your time.

I also recognize that you are each stepping into this journey at different points in your child's development. Some of you may have a child in elementary school just starting off in competitive sports. Others may have picked up this book because your freshman is all of a sudden being recruited to play collegiate athletics. I assure you, no matter your child's age or developmental level, there is plenty in this book you can apply to help your child thrive in their youth sports experience.

Another important note: though this book is written with you in mind, there is a lot in here that your daughter or son can benefit from. When they are old enough, encourage them to read with you. I will, at specific times, ask you to invite them to join you in some exercises (the non-physical kind) that will help them to consider important aspects of their athletic journey.[7]

Lastly, I want you to know you are not alone.

Yes, I am with you through the words of this book and in spirit, but there are also so many other parents trying to do their best to raise daughters and sons who also happen to be successful athletes. They are not that difficult to find. They are the parents sitting next to you in the stands. They are the ones a step ahead or a step behind.

---

7 **Note for Coaches:** There is so much in here that you too can learn and benefit from. In the back of this book you will find a Coaches' Appendix that will help you to consider how to best apply what this book has to offer to your very important profession.

I encourage you to find them and invite them to be a part of your team, to be a part of your support system as you become a part of theirs.

In the right context, sharing with your children in this journey can be one of the greatest honors of your entire life. I am so excited for you to unlock the joys that are to come.

CHAPTER 1

UNDERSTANDING YOUR ROLE

I attempted to hide my frustration from the group. We were only two games into the season and we were already having issues of disrespect and distraction. This team had a chance to be great. Every girl in it had the talent and the drive to play at the collegiate Division-I level. But I knew if we were going to succeed, we would have to work through this.

I had coached teams before, but it was rare that I needed to have this sort of post-game meeting this early on. A meeting not with the players, but with the parents.

Their fifth graders were actually amazing to coach! The kids worked hard in practice, paid close attention to the game plan, and supported their teammates well. It was no wonder they were able to play up a grade. But a number of these talented athletes' parents were causing problems during the game.

During the game, when trying to get a particular player's attention, I would often find her focus on the orders her parents were barking from the bleachers. What's worse is these instructions often would conflict with the game plan I went over with the players before the game. And it was not just one player's parents. It was like I had a chorus of misled coaches unintentionally undermining me at every turn.

At one point, I saw a parent walking opposite the bench where I was coaching, having a full conversation with his daughter *while she was in the game!*

Immediately after the game I called a parent meeting. I tactfully and patiently laid out the issues: (1) our team has a game plan that you as parents are not privy to, (2) you never know who may be scouting your daughters at any given game and what impact your actions might be having, and (3) you are modeling for your daughters a habit of disrespect towards me and future coaches.

They were of course apologetic, and I went on to greatly appreciate this particular group of parents. I knew they meant well and wanted to do what was right for their daughters. They just were a little misguided as to their role in their daughters' athletic journeys. That is why I always encourage no coaching from the bleachers.

Over my many years in youth sports, I've found it is deeply important to have a good grasp on what is and is not a helpful role for a parent to take in a child's athletic development. In this chapter, I want to help you fully understand how to approach your daughter or son's athletic journey from a place of health, care, and intentionality.

This can only come when we understand, first and foremost, our role as parents in our kids' lives.

Being a parent is the greatest honor—and greatest responsibility—we as human beings can receive. Over the course of our kids' lives we will play many roles. From tutor to mentor, cook to coach, we wear multiple hats and are constantly adapting to the many needs of our children.

Despite these numerous parts we play, the role of parent itself is paramount, transcending and eclipsing all else when it comes to our daughters and sons.

It is vital to keep this at the front of our minds as we consider how we will show up for our kids throughout their athletic journeys. Though it may seem like a no-brainer, take it from me, it is easy to get caught up in the task at hand or emotion of the moment. In this state we easily lose sight of our underlying goal as a parent. In this section, I want to offer four key objectives that should shape the way you interact with your child through the entirety of their athletic journeys.

When these objectives are given top priority, they will help to keep your role as a parent at the forefront of your mind.

OBJECTIVE 1: INSTILLING HEALTHY VALUES

Sports and athletic competition are incredible. They have the power to galvanize communities, teach deep truths, and bring hope and joy in difficult situations. In this way, sports are so much more than *just a game*. If we view our children's athletic journeys as ends unto themselves, we not only overlook the power of sports—we do our kids a disservice by not helping them get the most out of their youth sports experience.

So how do we wield this mighty instrument to support our task of raising healthy and whole individuals? How can we leverage sports as a healthy parenting tool to bring about greater good in our children's lives?

I want to suggest that the most helpful use of sports in a young person's life is as a vehicle for instilling values that will help them to succeed in life *beyond* sports. This is the first and primary objective of a parent who is raising a child who is an athlete.

Values are deeply held beliefs that shape the way a person interacts with the world around them. Instilling values through sports aligns greatly with our task as parents. This will be the objective I want you to aim for above all else.

Yes, you will learn to help them succeed in their respective sports, but I want you to keep your eyes on this greater end. Let's help your kids become successful lawyers, doctors, CEOs, and coaches. Let's teach them to be successful in relationships, to be good citizens, to be human beings of tremendous quality and character.

I would often tell my daughters that my primary concern in their lives was not basketball. What I really cared about was the way they represented themselves, our family, their team, and our community. I wanted them to know that who they were becoming mattered more to me than what they would accomplish.

My girls knew our family values: work hard at whatever you set out to accomplish, treat each person you encounter with respect, support and encourage your people (family, teammates, coaches, etc.), and always enjoy the process—just to name a few. I wanted my girls to have these values not only because I knew it would help their athletic careers, but because it would transfer to all aspects of their lives.

While coaching a group of sixth-grade girls, we ended up playing against one of the best players in the state. Our girls played hard and we ended up with the win. This incredible young athlete on the other team had an off-game by her standards, but still played well. After the game, I witnessed her father berating her in the parking lot as he slammed her gym bag into the trunk.

This is a perfect example of a father who has lost sight of his primary objective. Rather than teaching his daughter the core values that would help her in the future, he allowed his anger to teach his daughter that winning mattered more than respect, that her performance mattered more than enjoying the game.

Sadly, this is just one example of a far too common occurrence in gyms and fields across America. We all get frustrated, but we cannot let our emotions distract us from this vital objective. Our kids' futures depend on it!

So what are your family's values? And how do you plan on keeping them front and center? If you have not considered this before I encourage you to do so now. At the end of this chapter, you'll find a worksheet with a few questions to help you and your family solidify these values.

Once you have these values set, I encourage you to talk about them often as a family so as not to lose sight of what is truly important.

OBJECTIVE 2: BECOME A STUDENT OF YOUR CHILD

Every kid ticks differently and there is no cookie-cutter approach when it comes to a young athlete's development. When Jackie was growing up, our approach was shaped around her unique drive, goals, and way of learning. Our training sessions together were hyper-focused and productive, because that fit with Jackie's personality. In under an hour, she had already hit her target goal for shots made.

Early in her development we went for four hundred makes at a 70% clip. By the time she was a senior in high school she was hitting upwards of five hundred shots at that percentage in the same amount of time. Girl could just flat-out shoot!

As a young dad who also was a recovering perfectionist, I used to push Jackie the same way I liked to be pushed as an athlete. I'd correct her after every shot and keep going beyond the time limit I knew she was accustomed to. I knew studies had shown that it took repeating something three times for it to set in a person's brain, and so I put that knowledge into practice.

I was yet to learn how a father's repeated badgering annoys his daughters to no end.

As a result, our early training sessions would often end with us both frustrated with each other. I had to learn that Jackie was not me, and she was not any other athlete I had encountered. She had unique needs and I was foolish to try to push things on her that just did not fit her personality.

I had to become a student of my child, otherwise the process was not going to be enjoyable for either of us. This meant learning when to stop and learning when to keep my mouth shut. Eventually, we found our groove together and these training sessions were a connecting point for our relationship.

Later, Jaime would benefit from a bit older and a bit wiser version of Dad. Even though they grew up with the same parents, Jaime and Jackie's athletic development and the way they went about their work was completely different. Jaime would stay in the gym for upwards of two hours. She was on a mission to make it to the WNBA and she was going to do whatever it took to get there. I adapted the way I showed up for Jaime based on who she was as a person and what she was going after.

If we want to truly help our kids achieve their dreams, if we hope to use sports to help instill in them values to serve them for a lifetime, then we must be humble enough to connect with our daughters and sons on their terms. This means we all have to become students of our children, learning what resonates with them as individuals and what sort of environment is best for their unique development. This is our second key objective.

Another side of this same coin is knowing yourself, how you will respond to certain things, how you communicate, and what your limitations are. We have to come to terms with the fact that there is only so much we can teach our children when it comes to athletics.

For me, the test came when my daughters left high school to play on the collegiate level. I knew it was time for them to get different trainers who could take them to another level. For some of you this transition may happen earlier on, because you did not play the sport at that level yourself. Either way, having multiple trusted voices helping your child's athletic development is a good thing that you should welcome.

(We will talk more about trainers and when to hire outside help in chapter five.)

But as your role in their development shifts, be looking for ways to stay involved and continue to be a student of your kid as they grow. Remember that your objective is bigger than their success in sports. In these seasons, shift your focus to these greater things.

Help them to understand themselves. Teach them to know their limits, when they need to push themselves and when they need to rest. Model and help them set up good boundaries. Show them how to handle their own schedule and teach them to live a balanced and healthy life.

And in all this, continue to guide them to greater levels of success, keeping in mind that you are first and foremost a parent hoping to leverage the power of sports to instill in your child values that will serve them in life.

OBJECTIVE 3: HELP THEM SET GOALS

A huge part of being a student of your child is taking the intentional time to help them map out their athletic goals before the start of each new season. A goal is different from a dream. A *dream* is a big-picture vision your child uses to drive them forward and help them persevere through difficulty. *Goals*, on the other hand, are short-term, achievable objectives within one's control that support that greater dream.

Though goal-setting conversations are extremely beneficial for young athletes, these conversations are actually intended primarily to help *you*, as a parent, better know your child. If you understand your daughter or son's goal for a given season, you are far better equipped to support them in achieving that goal. Take Tyler for example:

Tyler is a seventh grader with a love for soccer and a dream to play on the collegiate level. Over the last year he has taken a tremendous leap in athleticism and skill, making an elite club team in the area. Tyler's parents are excited about their son's growth, and sit down with him to help him plan his athletic goals for the summer going into eighth grade. They are somewhat surprised when Tyler informs them that he would like to only play for his school team this summer, and not train with the elite club during his break from school.

Tyler's parents inform him that many of his teammates train year around, and his decision may cost him his starting position on the elite club come the fall. After some thought, Tyler informs his parents that, though he still dreams to play collegiately, he knows that the following summer will bring a new level of seriousness, as he will be preparing for high school athletics. In preparation for the hard work that is ahead of him, he would like to take this summer to "just enjoy soccer" and remember why he loves the game.

Knowing Tyler understands both the benefits and costs of his decision, they support him and ask him how they can help him to achieve his goal of enjoying soccer over the summer.

This is an example of a healthy goal setting with a young athlete. Though Tyler's parents think they know what Tyler's goals are for the summer season, they take the time to sit down and have the conversation with him anyway.

When Tyler's goals do not seem to align with his dream of playing soccer collegiately, they patiently help Tyler weigh the costs and benefits that his summer goal might have on this dream. When Tyler's parents see that his goal is well thought-out, they support his decision and ask him how they can help him achieve that goal.

One of the primary ways we as parents lose track of our greater parental purpose is to put our own dreams and goals for our kids ahead of the dreams and goals they have for themselves. This unhealthy approach to your child's athletic journey is easier to slip into than you may think. Regular goal-setting conversations help to prevent us as parents from commandeering this journey, and can help us to support our children in *their* dreams and goals.

Now make no mistake, the greater the dream, the harder the work. It is important that we are tactfully and graciously honest with our kids about their dreams and if the goals they are setting will in fact help them to get there. You do not need to be overly harsh, but they need to understand that if they want to continue to grow as an athlete, they will need to put in the necessary work.

As Hall of Fame football coach Vince Lombardi once said, "The only place that success comes before work is in the dictionary."

At the end of this chapter, you will find a *Goal-Setting Worksheet* for you to recreate with your child each time you have a goal-setting conversation. I encourage you to set goals with your child twice a year: before the school season and before each select-ball or club season.

OBJECTIVE 4: BE THEIR BIGGEST CHEERLEADER

I hesitate to put this objective last, as it is as important, if not more important, than some of the other objectives in this chapter. As parents our words, moods, and even facial expressions can have a huge impact on our daughters and sons.

All athletes have good days and bad days. The way a parent responds to these can shift the confidence of an athlete for the next three or four games. An offhand comment or disapproving look, though we may forget about it soon after, can cut deep into a child's heart. This is why it is vital that we as parents are thoughtful and intentional encouragers of our children.

There are plenty of critics in the world. What your child needs is a *cheerleader*. Someone they know will be in their corner and have their back no matter what. It is vital that we as parents approach every aspect of our child's athletic journey with this perspective.

When they are training, notice and mention their improvements. Before the games, let them know you are excited to watch them play. Remember a couple things they have been working on throughout the week and encourage them in those areas.

During the game, simply allow your kid to play. Only use your voice to cheer and support. Trust me, your critiques are not helpful to them at this moment. Pay attention to your body language and facial expressions. If they look at you in the stands, give a clap and shout of encouragement. If your kid believes you are disappointed it can derail them for the entire game.

And please, leave the coaching to the coach. Just because a coach is being paid does not give anyone the right to undermine or disrespect them.

Your response after the game is perhaps the most important, especially if your daughter or son played poorly. There are so many emotions an athlete feels after a game, most of which they will not want to share in that moment.

The Positive Coaching Alliance (an organization whose resources I highly recommend) taught me that it is best in this time to give your child space to process the game. They will bring up the game if and when they are ready. With my daughters, I would simply say the same thing every time they got in the car after a game: "I enjoyed watching you play."

And that was always true. Win or loss, I saw it as a privilege and joy to watch my daughters play the game they loved.

After that, if they brought up the game, we would talk about it. But I left the choice to them. In the case they did want to talk, I would be conscious of my tone and strive to be calm and positive. I would start by highlighting two or three things that they did well. Since most athletes focus on the negative, this helps them to have a more balanced outlook on their performance.

If the conversation came to it, we would talk about one or two areas I thought they could improve on before the next game.

I learned to be careful with my words here though, as an overly harsh word can take the wind out of a young athlete's sails. I focused on things they could control, such as how hard they worked, their form, the way they showed up for their teammates, etc. Using the phrase "I think you might be able to improve on…" presents a more optimistic outlook and gives them an action step before the next game. This is more favorable than language such as "You played poorly because…" or "You really didn't do a good job of…"

I cannot stress how important it is that your kids feel supported and encouraged by you as their parent. You showing up as your daughter or son's greatest cheerleader is vital to helping them grow as an athlete and as a healthy person.

A FINAL NOTE: THE COMMITMENT WE MAKE AS PARENTS

Over the years, I have grown close with Tiger Woods and his family. (Sorry to name-drop—working at Nike for over fifteen years has its benefits.) In that time, Tiger's mother, Tida, has become a dear friend and like a second mother to me. I would often ask her not only how Tiger became such a huge success, but also how they as parents helped make Tiger's athletic journey special for him as he was growing up. This especially interested me because I hoped to make my girls' sports journeys just as special.

I remember her once saying, "When kids start having success in sports, they will want more. You have to be sure you are ready for more as well." Indeed my girls did want more. As their success grew, so did their desire to have more sports in their young lives.

More practice, *more* training, to be around the game *more*. And all along the way they needed more from us as parents. *More* rides, *more* attention, *more* support. Tida's point was clear: in order for my girls to achieve what they hoped, they needed their mom and me to be just as committed as they were. They needed us in it with them.

The four objectives outlined in this chapter will help you to be with your child through the ups and downs of their athletic journey. This will demand a lot of you. Helping your children chase everything that athletics has to offer takes a tremendous amount of work, energy, and time on your part. Not to mention the financial investment.

Before diving any further into this book, I want you to understand all you are getting—or perhaps already have gotten—into.

That said, I also want you to know that it is worth it! All of those difficulties pale in comparison to the amazing honor it is to help the ones most precious to you go after their dreams.

FAMILY VALUES WORKSHEET

As a whole family, talk through the questions below and come up with five family values. Family values are ways of living that help you all remember to be the best you can be. Parents, make sure the whole family is involved and you help younger kids understand what a value is so that they can best participate. Each value should be summed up with one or two words that are easy to remember and a short phrase that describes what the value means (e.g., "Respect: Have respect for each person we meet").

- *When other people think of our family, we want them to think of how _____ we are.*
- *When thinking about the goals we have as a family, what traits would serve us best?*
- *When things get tough, what values do we want to have as a family to get us through?*

Below are the Nared family values as an example. Some of these family values I am going to recommend you adopt as your own, as they will serve your family and children well.

OUR FIVE FAMILY VALUES: **THE NARED FAMILY**				
RESPECT	HIGH CHARACTER	GROWTH MINDSET	GRATEFULNESS	WORK ETHIC
Have respect for each person we meet.	How we act and treat people matters. Always do things the right way. Don't deviate.	Understand ourselves and others as valuable.	Approach our lives grateful for all the blessings we have.	Work at whatever we do.

OUR FIVE FAMILY VALUES:				
VALUE #1	VALUE #2	VALUE #3	VALUE #4	VALUE #5
Description	Description	Description	Description	Description

GOAL-SETTING WORKSHEET

Have your daughter or son re-create the worksheet on the next page on a separate piece of paper each time they set goals for the season.[8] *Additionally, your children can re-create a separate worksheet as they consider their academic dreams and goals for the school year, or their relational dreams and goals with family and friends for the upcoming school year.*

---

8 Recommended for athletes sixth grade and above.

THE DREAM: *What is your big-picture vision for your sports/academic/relational journey? This is what you will use to drive you forward and help you persevere through difficulty.*

THE DREAM

YOUR GOALS: *What are three goals for the next season/school year that can help you take one step closer to this dream? Write how each of those goals will help you step closer to your dream.*
NOTE: *Goals should be:*

* *short-term (something you can accomplish within the next season)*
* *achievable (something realistic and measurable),*
* *within your control (batting .500 for the season—i.e., getting on base 50% of the time— is out of your control; taking one thousand quality swings at the batting cages once a week is within your control).*

1	2	3

CHAPTER 2

BUILDING ON A FOUNDATION OF RESPECT

I walked with my daughter Jaime—who had donned her cap and gown—through the halls of her University of Tennessee dorm, which she had called home for her junior and senior years.

I remember being so impressed with my youngest. Yes, I was blown away by all she had achieved both academically and athletically, but what stood out to me more was the way my daughter interacted with everyone we passed in the hallways. From classmates to custodians, everyone knew her name and she knew theirs in return.

"We are going to miss you so much, Jaime," one of the custodians said to her. Another stopped us to tell Jaime how much they loved her. My daughter had grown into someone who was enjoyed and respected highly by all those around her, and I couldn't have been more proud.

When I consider how Jaime garnered—and continues to garner—such a high level of respect from all those around her, it doesn't take long to discover her secret. She is a person that is deeply intentional about offering incredible respect to everyone she encounters.

Respect is valuing someone or something with proper regard. Sometimes, we approach respect as something that someone else has to earn from us. This is true in a way. If you want me to respect your three-point shot, you have to show me you can make it. If you want me to respect that you are true to your word, you have to follow through. But there is a certain level of respect that we should offer each person we encounter, no matter the situation.

Jackie Robinson once said, "I'm not concerned with your liking or disliking me. All I ask is that you respect me as a human being." In this he highlighted the fundamental truth that every person deserves the respect garnered simply from being human.

Perhaps this seems obvious to you, but given the way we treat each other in this world, it is something I feel compelled to discuss. To respect someone's humanity is to value them enough to treat them with kindness, to acknowledge them as visible, to listen and seek to understand where they are coming from.

Yet we so often approach one another with a callousness or even cruelty. We ignore others, treating individuals as though they were invisible. We become so self-consumed that we can only see things our way and lack basic empathy for others. We are all guilty of this kind of blatant disrespect, me included.

What is more terrifying is the cycle this sends our world into. Disrespect only begets more disrespect, and thus is corrosive to our families, communities, and society as a whole.

This is exactly why we need to strive to live differently and teach our children to do the same. The only way to short-circuit a cycle of disrespect is for someone to choose to respond to disrespect with respect instead. Imagine how transformative that could be!

As parents, my daughters' mother and I made modeling respect a huge priority. We wanted our daughters to see every human as possessing inherent value and thus deserving a certain level of regard.

We would have been lying to ourselves if we thought we could teach it without living it.

This is going to be a common theme throughout this book. If you are not willing to live the values you desire to impart to your children, you can count on being minimally effective. If we shout and cuss at officials at our children's games, do you believe our children will grow to be people who treat officials with respect? If we bad-mouth their coach on the drive home, how will they respond to that same coach in practice or a game? If we operate with constant disrespect when it comes to our own families, can we really expect our kids to go out and be agents of respect in the world?

This is challenging, but, as it is with all things we seek to impart with our children, it has to start with us. We do not have to be perfect at this—I know I am certainly not—but it should be something we are striving for.

Respect is absolutely indispensable for your child's athletic journey. As you consider your family's values, I want to propose to you that respect is what is most fundamental to setting your child up for success in chasing their dreams.

Respect is the base that the entire system in this book is built on.

RESPECT YOURSELF

A really amazing organization that I have been involved in for many years is the Positive Coaching Alliance. They are, in their own words, "a national non-profit developing Better Athletes, Better People through youth and high school sports."⁹ They have a number of incredible resources for players, parents, and coaches that are more than worth checking out. One of these resources is called ROOTS. With this resource, PCA hopes to help youth sports become a place characterized by honor— honor for people, of course, but also a place where the game, rules, and process are honored. They hope to do this by "better respecting: Rules, Opponents, Officials, Teammates and Self."¹⁰

In this chapter, I want to highlight an element of respect I think often is overlooked: respect for self. According to PCA, an athlete's respect for self is the most important element of these ROOTS of honoring the game. This is because in order to offer respect to others, our daughters and sons must have a well of deep self-respect to draw from.

Self-respect comes first from a child having a stable and healthy relationship with their parents. We have to teach and show our children how valuable they are through our time, encouragement, guidance, and belief in them. We have to remind them of their value and not allow others to make them feel less valuable.

9 "PCA Development Zone®," PCA Development Zone®, Positive Coaching Alliance, accessed March 21, 2021, https://devzone.positivecoach.org/.

10 "The ROOTS Of Honoring The Game And Sportsmanship," PCA Development Zone®, accessed March 21, 2021, https://devzone.positivecoach.org/resource/book/roots-honoring-game-and-sportsmanship#:~:text=%E2%80%9CHonoring%20the%20Game%E2%80%9D%20is%20a,%2C%20Officials%2C%20Teammates%20and%20Self.

Next, we have to teach them the importance of building habits of self-respect. Self-respect looks like teaching our kids to care for their bodies, minds, and souls. It means doing what might be difficult in the moment in order to experience more joy in the long run. It means having healthy boundaries and not allowing others to overstep those boundaries. It means believing in themselves and having the confidence to chase after the goals and dreams that they have laid before themselves.

Self-respect will also help our children to prioritize what they are seeking from others. All-time-great basketball legend Julius "Dr. J" Erving once said, "I firmly believe that respect is a lot more important, and a lot greater, than popularity." What Erving realized is that seeking to earn a person's respect is a far better goal than trying to be liked by everyone. The person who wants to be liked by everyone is likely drawing from a deficit of self-respect. This kind of person is willing to do almost anything just to be liked by others. They will jeopardize their values, and are more likely to disrespect—treat with less value—themselves and others for the sake of feeling more liked.

This is especially important for a successful athlete who will be well-liked and earn the attention of others at some point. There is an important but subtle difference between self-respect and pride, self-confidence and arrogance. Pride and arrogance involve the need to be seen, acknowledged by others. Pride and arrogance grow from a deficit of self-respect, and the proud and arrogant person is desperate for others to notice their greatness.

When drawing from a deep sense of self-respect, our daughters and sons can live from a place of internal confidence and approach their athletic journeys secure in themselves and the family values we have instilled. Others will respect them for it—treat them with the value they deserve—because they are secure in who they are, not easily swayed by the world around them.

This will only get more difficult as they grow and garner more attention from others for their athletic achievements. It is important that we as parents help our kids understand this subtle difference, and have conversations with them about self-respect at an early age.

We will be reviewing many of these themes in the chapters to come, but I could not move forward without touching on this topic.

RESPECT OTHERS

The greatest teams in the history of sports are built on a culture of respect. From the team manager or the custodian in the gym, all the way up to the head coach, teams who want long-lasting success make mutual respect a priority. If your daughter or son wants to be a part of such a team, they will need to learn to respect others.

Disrespect can take a few different forms. The most obvious form is allowing anger or frustration to cause us to treat others with unkindness. Not only is our role as parents to model respect for our children, but it is also to call out disrespect when we see it.

Take Jazmin for example:

Jazmin is a sixth-grade lacrosse player who has excelled in the sport as a defender—so much so that she has been invited to practice a few grades up on the eighth-grade team. Jazmin is quick, but on the eighth-grade team there are some girls that can keep up with her on the field and even get the better of her. This frustrates Jazmin, and her parents notice that she even yells at the coach when the coach tries to correct her technique. As a result, her coach benches her to cool off.

After practice, Jazmin's parents ask her about the incident. Jazmin says that she already knew what the coach was trying to tell her and it wouldn't have helped her any. Jazmin's parents understand her frustration, but are not okay with the disrespect she showed her coach by losing her cool. They talk with her about apologizing to her coach and how to handle her frustration better in the future.

Jazmin's parents could have easily allowed her coach to be the only one to address the situation, but they noticed that Jazmin acted outside their family's value of respect for each person. Their correction of their daughter had less to do with sports and more to do with the kind of person they want her to grow into.

We as parents should be thinking this way continuously. We have a responsibility to help shape our children into people of respect. This happens in the little conversations and corrections along the way.

It would be an oversight for me to not also talk about how this form of disrespect is prevalent online among young people. Technology is a powerful tool and it allows us to communicate and make connections like never before. But like fire, this tool that can be so helpful can also burn your children or others if it is not used with discernment.

Whether it is social media, online gaming, streaming, chat rooms, or private messages and the like, being online can cause people to do and say things that they would never do or say if they were interacting in person. Though these actions often feel harmless, they can have a dramatic effect on others and on our kids. Thus we as parents need to have conversations about having a responsible and respectful online presence. We also need to stay locked in with our children's online presence, having a grasp on where they go, who they interact with, how they interact, and what they say.

Help your kids understand the power of their words and posts online. Help them understand that inappropriate, unkind, or hateful words or posts are deeply disrespectful to everyone that happens to see them. Help them understand that sending lewd or unseemly messages is not showing proper respect for themselves or the person they are sending it to. Discuss with them how everything they do and post online is tracked, never truly disappears, and can be used against them later in their lives. Talk to them about the dangers of online communication and how to protect themselves from those who might be looking to take advantage of them.

This is a huge piece of our children's world these days, so if you do not understand the online world, I urge you to do research and get informed.

Disrespect is not always as blatant as a shouting outburst or obviously obscene comment online, however. Sometimes it presents itself in more passive ways and involves ignoring, excluding, or simply not acknowledging other people.

I find youth employ this kind of disrespect quite frequently. It still boggles my mind how two athletes can be super friendly at practice and then walk past each other in the halls at school without so much as a hello. Team text messages are started without a few key members. Get-togethers are planned with a couple players excluded. Cliques are formed and make others feel like they are less-valued members of the team.

Though this is subtle, it shows others incredible disrespect and can be terribly damaging to a team culture. It is vital that we teach our kids the importance of inclusion, and the basic social skills of being friendly to those they know and showing the decency of acknowledging them. We must teach them how impactful it can be to look someone in the eye and genuinely listen to how they are doing.

My daughter Jackie was great at this in high school. Her friend group consisted of approximately everybody. It helped that she is just a fun and incredible person to be around, but she also made time for people, even if social norms suggested she could ignore them. She was popular, and a talented athlete, but she made time to care about those whom the cutthroat culture of high school said she didn't need to notice.

Now some of your kids will be more introverted, so we don't need to force them all to have a large friend group, but we do want to teach them to treat everyone they encounter *as a friend.*

By being a friend, they show each person the level of respect that all people deserve.

Simultaneously, they will be serving themselves. When they treat others this way, they will find that more people like to be around them. They will become someone who most others respect in a similar fashion. Not only that, but a person who respects others intentionally is a huge asset to any team culture—something all good coaches recognize.

Though your sons and daughters cannot shape a team culture all on their own, sometimes this sort of hyper-intentional respect can be contagious. It is a catalyst that can shift a culture for the better, just like a single disrespectful person can change a culture for the worse. Coaches love to keep these sorts of respectful teammates around, especially when they are talented and hardworking.

And the best part is that they do not have to lose their edge at all. One of the greatest tennis pros of all time, Roger Federer, lives by the mantra, "I fear no one, but respect everyone." Encourage your kids to be competitive, hardworking, and self-confident, all while treating others with the highest respect, valuing them as human beings.

It is also important to teach our daughters and sons to respect others even when it is difficult to do so. You do not have to even like someone to treat them with respect. Sometimes we have teammates, coaches, and opponents that just rub us the wrong way, or treat us unfairly or unkindly for no apparent reason. When this happens, respect becomes all the more important, as it can help break the cycle of disrespect that we have already mentioned.

That said, this does not mean that we should allow our kids to be mistreated or that these conflicts should simply be swept under the rug. That would show lack of respect for our own children and also would not be teaching them to respect themselves. Instead, respect looks like bringing things up to a person in a calm and kind manner and allowing them the chance to change their behavior. People of respect are not doormats by any means. In fact, they are usually far more admired and venerated for their strength, security, and calm when faced with relational challenges.

None of this is easy, and the world will try to influence our children to live from a place of insecurity and deficit. Their popularity will try to tell them that they should take and hold onto attention rather than offer kindness to others. It will say that they should find ways to raise their own status and position rather than looking to serve and elevate others.

It is vital that we communicate to them that this ultimately is a losing strategy for both life and sports. The adage "the best players are the ones who make their teammates better" will serve them not only all along their athletic journey, but also will serve them in being a better friend, daughter or son, employee, boss, spouse, and parent.

Though they cannot control how others choose to live, if we teach our kids to strive to embrace this kind of lifestyle of respect, they will find that the more respect they give out, the more they will receive in return.

RESPECT THE GAME

Another huge element of respect that we must discuss before moving on is respect for the game. An athlete cannot become truly successful if they do not learn to have a special regard for the game they desire to play and what it can offer them when leveraged properly.

Veteran MLB infielder, Asdrúbal Cabrera, talked about respect for the game while starting on a new team a few years back. He said, "More than anything, you have to respect the game and do things the right way. I feel like that's why the team and the staff here respect me."[11]

Cabrera talks about "doing things the right way." This is a key element of respecting the game. Athletes who look for shortcuts to get ahead, operate outside the rules, and try to circumvent the hard work that is necessary to grow into a truly successful athlete and person of character will struggle to engage with the process that is laid out in this book. There is no substitution for putting in the necessary hours and effort it requires to be great.

Everything you read from here on out is built on this principle. This sort of respect—for self, others, and the game—will launch your child far beyond the dreams of their youth and into an immensely wonderful and satisfying life.

11 Maria Guardado, "As Mets Continue Playoff Push, Cabrera Soldiers On," NJ.com, NJ Advance Media, September 25, 2016, https://www.nj.com/mets/2016/09/as_mets_continue_playoff_push_asdrubal_cabrera_sol.html.

CHAPTER 3

PATHWAYS TO GREATNESS

When you think of athletes who have achieved greatness, who comes to mind? Serena? MJ? Rapinoe? Tiger? Taurasi? Though each of these athletes walked their own unique journey on the way to achieving athletic success, there are some characteristics they share—some pathways common to each and all of them that helped to pave their way towards greatness. I want to help your daughters and sons embrace some of these same pathways in order to achieve their own versions of greatness.

Now will they become the next Simone Biles or Mike Trout? Unlikely. These sorts of athletic journeys are once in a generation.

As one of the greatest coaches in the history of sports, John Wooden, once said, "Success is peace of mind which is a direct result of self-satisfaction in knowing you did your best to become the best you are capable of becoming."

As the UCLA great implies, greatness is not about becoming someone else, but about becoming the absolute best version of yourself.

There are four pathways to greatness that I want to highlight in this chapter: *love, loyalty, hunger,* and *humility.* When these pathways are walked with integrity and intentionality, not only can they bring about greatness in sports, but they also are able to manifest greatness in our daughters' or sons' lives.

When we help them to transition to utilizing these pathways off the field or the court, we will see our kids become far more than great athletes: they will become great employees, great bosses, great citizens. What's more, they will have the tools to move with great courage, kindness, and perseverance in their relationships, so that they may be great friends, great spouses and great parents.

This is true greatness because its benefits will not stop with our children but will radiate towards everyone they encounter. Coretta Scott King once said, "The greatness of a community is most accurately measured by the compassionate actions of its members." Though we are going to be talking about these four pathways in the context of sports, King's understanding of greatness is what we should be pursuing for our children and our world.

Let us not lose sight of this reality.

LOVE OF THE GAME

Hall of Fame soccer legend Mia Hamm once wrote, "Somewhere behind the athlete you've become and the hours of practice and the coaches who have pushed you is a little girl who fell in love with the game and never looked back ... play for her."[12]

There is such wisdom in her words. Having a genuine love for your craft cannot be undersold when it comes to pushing through difficulty on one's way to greatness. This first pathway, *to discover,*

---

12 Mia Hamm and Aaron Heifetz, *Go for the Goal: A Champion's Guide to Winning in Soccer and Life* (New York, NY: Quill, 2002).

foster, and maintain a love of the game, is something that successful athletes point to as an indispensable ingredient to achieving greatness.

Though I use the words *foster* and *maintain,* I do not want to mislead you in any way. Love of a particular sport cannot be fabricated or faked. It has to start with joy, something that can only be *discovered* through trial and error. But when joy is discovered, it is like a seed. It has near miraculous potential for growth and can bear fruit that feels like merely a dream considering where it started.

That said, if a seed is to grow, it must be given a healthy environment and provided with what is necessary. Before we get too far ahead, though, let's consider more of how we can encourage discovery of a love for sports within our children.

When my girls were young, I encouraged them to try lots of sports, and lots of positions within each sport. Even though my greatest love was basketball, I knew it was important not to try to force this love on my daughters. It is normal for us as parents to desire a common love for our children and us to share together, but sometimes we can create a plan for our kids' lives based on what we love, rather than what we find they love.

If basketball was going to be the sport that took hold of my daughters' hearts, it needed to come about naturally. So I encouraged my daughters to play basketball, soccer, volleyball, tennis, and to run track. What's more, within each sport they took on different roles and tried different positions so that they could discover what brought them the most passion and joy. This is because the main way our daughters and sons will discover their pathway is through actually getting out there and trying lots of different athletic endeavors.

As you'll read about in the chapters to come, I am a big fan of multisport athletics and the numerous benefits it brings, especially for elementary-age children.

Once you have helped your kids to discover love for a sport, you can help them foster that love to maturity. This process is mainly giving your kids the opportunity to see and experience all that sport has to offer. This means playing with your kid and teaching them to have fun. Show them how it can feel to be truly blessed by sports and what it is like to take fun seriously.

If our kids are to have a dream of what can come from sports, we also have to give them a vision of what their future can look like. This means going to games at a local high school or college—community colleges are a great option if a big university is not nearby—and introducing them to athletes that are a step ahead. It means rooting for their favorite team with them and encouraging their interests. Early on, you may be doing this for multiple sports as your kids find where their passions truly lie. Again, letting these passions grow naturally is important if they are to be maintained.

You will know that love is mature when your daughter or son is the one fighting to feed this growing passion of theirs. They will be the ones shooting the ball until it is too dark to see, waking up early to watch Wimbledon live, or dragging you to *another* dance competition.

And though this fostered love for the game can get your kids through great difficulty in their athletic journey, it is not indestructible. The final step in solidifying this pathway is teaching your child to maintain and protect it.

Athletes lose love of the game for so many different reasons. If a sport is played at an overwhelming rate over an entire childhood, burnout is likely to occur. This is especially true when an athlete does not intentionally take extended breaks away from the sport. (You will read more about rest and taking time off in the chapters to come.)

Another way loss of love can fester in an athlete's sports journey is through repeated discouragement. This may come through an overly harsh parent or coach. I, like all parents, have been guilty of being too harsh with my kids, but—like I mentioned in the first chapter—we are fooling ourselves if we believe that this harshness, *when it becomes a pattern*, does not have a devastating effect on our children's confidence and self-esteem.

A favorite proverb of mine says, "Gentle words are a tree of life; a deceitful tongue crushes the spirit."[13] This proverb reminds me of the power of my words to give life or to crush spirits. Because of this, it is important to make age-appropriate critiques and to emphasize encouragement with your kids. Also make sure that when your kids are young you are entrusting them to coaches that are positive but not afraid to be constructive and teach as well.

As your daughter or son gets older, they will have less control over who coaches them. That is why it is also good to have conversations with them about how to work hard and deal with conflict even when they are in a less than ideal situation. In this, they will

13 Proverbs 15:4, NLT Bible.

learn to take constructive criticism as an invitation to get better. It is important then to show them that no matter how fair or encouraging the coach, there is always space to learn, grow, and show up the right way.

Another common discouragement can come through repeated or serious injury. Like burnout, this often comes with an over-whelming sports schedule and not prioritizing rest. According to an article from *Nationwide Children's Hospital of Sports Medicine*,

> sports injuries are the second leading cause of emergency room visits for children and adolescents, and the second leading cause of injuries in school. Approximately three million youth are seen in hospital emergency rooms for sports-related injuries and another five million youth are seen by their primary care physician or a sports medicine clinic for injuries.[14]

These injuries not only have an impact on our children's young psyches, but also on their future ability to be active. One study reports,

> ACL injuries are becoming increasingly common among young athletes, particularly young women in the 15–19-year age group … A major problem after an ACL injury is that, regardless of treatment, athletes with the injury retire from active

---

14 "Kid's Sports Injuries: The Numbers Are Impressive," NationWideChildrens. org, Nationwide Children's Hospital, accessed March 24, 2021, https://www. nationwidechildrens.org/specialties/sports-medicine/sports-medicine-articles/ kids-sports-injuries-the-numbers-are-impressive.

participation at a higher rate than athletes without this injury. In one study, 80% of soccer players reported reduced activity levels 14 years after ACL injury. These outcomes are usually due to residual knee instability, reduced range of motion and/ or stiffness and pain.[15]

Love of the game is not possible if they are sidelined and potentially limited even beyond their youth. This is why we must do all we can to ensure proper rest and health practices in our young athletes. This is just one way that we can protect the passions of our young people so that they may learn to foster love for whatever dreams they set their minds to.

Finally, love for the game is protected when your kid learns to enjoy the process. The trailblazing tennis great Arthur Ashe once said, "Success is a journey, not a destination. The doing is often more important than the outcome." Let's teach our kids to enjoy life and sports in the moment. It holds true that the present is the only place that life can truly be lived.

LOYALTY MATTERS

Another vital pathway towards greatness in one's athletic journey is *loyalty*. Sadly, we are seeing loyalty dwindle in our culture, especially in the sports world. These days, there seems to be a growing disregard for the value of a commitment and how one's

---

15 N. Maffulli, U. G. Longo, N. Gougoulias, M. Loppini, V. Denaro, "Long-term health outcomes of youth sports injuries," Journal of Sports Medicine (2010): 21–25, http://citeseerx. ist.psu.edu/viewdoc/download?doi=10.1.1.982.3745&rep=rep1&type=pdf.

decisions impact others. From youth sports to the pros, athletes and teams alike move on from each other without batting an eye. Take Erin's situation for example:

Erin is a talented defenseman on her high school hockey team. Now a sophomore, she has been called up to the varsity team, where the game is faster and the talent level higher. Despite all her hard work in the off-season, her varsity coach gives her little playing time. One day, Erin comes home from practice visibly frustrated. Her dad, Brandon, inquires as to what is wrong and Erin tells her father that she wants to quit the team. Erin tells her dad that even though she is working as hard as anyone on the team (if not working even harder), her coach won't allow her to move into the rotation. She even tries to talk her dad into having her transferred to the school across town, since the varsity coach at that rival school coached Erin in peewee hockey.

Brandon reminds his daughter of the commitment she made to her teammates and the coach that she is currently frustrated with. He then asks her how her coach responded when Erin asked him about her playing time. Erin admits that she has not actually talked to the coach about her frustration. Working together, Brandon helps his daughter come up with a plan to calmly ask her coach what she might do to break into the regular rotation.

Though Erin changing teams would not be the greatest betrayal of all time, her father helping her to practice things now, while the stakes are relatively low, will be of huge benefit to her later, when the stakes are much higher. At the core, Brandon is teaching his daughter the importance of loyalty.

Loyalty is the chosen quality of enduring allegiance shared between two or more people for the sake of a greater good.

Our loyalty to others communicates that they matter to us, that we consider them in our choices, and care about how they are affected by our decisions.

Though loyalty is a wonderful trait in and of itself, with it you also gain an arsenal of positive qualities. A loyal person will learn to persevere through difficulty, recognize challenges as an opportunity for growth, build integrity, and learn to communicate through conflict in a healthy way. You just never know what seeing something through with a person or group might bring.

As a freshman at the University of Maryland, I loved my student-athlete experience. My teammates were great, my coaches were great, and I was living out my dream of playing basketball at a high level.

That is, until sophomore year rolled around and we got a new head coach. This new coach and I meshed about as well as oil and water. It felt like we clashed at every turn. It seemed like he was on a mission to get me to transfer schools. He was constantly on my back in practice, and blaming and harassing me for no reason all season long—which was unusual for someone who was not a starter. After my sophomore year, I was furious and seriously considered transferring.

I decided against it. *I'm not going to allow this guy to steal my joy of the game*, I thought. My junior year was more of the same, with the two of us clashing on a regular basis. We did not see eye to eye. Despite my anger and frustration, I worked hard to never disrespect this coach and tried to do all that was asked of me.

The two of us had to work through our differences as I ended up in his starting lineup and as a serious contributor as a senior. I cannot say that we had a perfect relationship that final year, but we found a way to respect each other and as a result grinded through the year. I did not think much on how my loyal actions would affect me in the future.

A couple years after graduation, I was applying for a dream job to work with professional athletes on the sports marketing team at Nike. Those hiring me did their due diligence and reached out to those who had worked closely with me, one of which was my coach from the University of Maryland.

I was surprised to hear that this coach who I had clashed with for three long years had given me the highest recommendation possible for the position. In his letter of reference, my old coach highlighted how hard I worked, how respectful I was, and how I would run through a wall for my team.

I can say without a doubt that my persevering loyalty at the University of Maryland changed my life. It is possible that I would not be in the position I am today without my coach's glowing reference.

Now I am not saying that there is never a good reason to leave a team. Abusive coaches on both the physical and verbal level, toxic team cultures, and untenable misalignment of values are a few important reasons to move on.

But if these things do not seem to be present, I encourage you to help your daughter or son to take their time in making a decision as major as whether or not to leave a team.

Here is a helpful process when your child is considering changing teams:

1. Go watch your child's team practice three or four times. Pay attention to how they are showing up. Are they giving the energy and focus needed? Are they being a good teammate? How is their attitude in practice? Are they disrespectful to the coach and/or others? All these can be reasons that a conflict exists. Also, be really observant at your kids' games, asking the same sort of questions. You may be able to help them solve the problem without further conversation.

2. If the problem persists, help them come up with a plan to communicate in a calm, healthy manner with their coach about the conflict they are experiencing. If they are in eighth grade or below, I recommend going with them. If they are in high school, it is time for them to have these conversations on their own. This will help them to prepare for future conflicts in college and beyond that you will not be able to bail them out of. If the situation escalates in an unhealthy way, you can then, of course, step in.

3. If the situation is still untenable, sit down with your kid and try to figure out why this is so. Consider the pros and cons of staying with the team as opposed to leaving. Ask questions that help them to think through how this will impact their teammates, coaches, and self.

Unfortunately, it has become commonplace for conflicts to cause rifts that selflessness and proper communication could easily remedy. Let's change that trend in our kids' lives!

HUNGER FOR GROWTH

Hunger is hard to teach, but it is also a pathway that cannot be circumvented if greatness is to be achieved. It is hunger that makes a great athlete, not talent. As Derek Jeter famously said, "There may be people that have more talent than you, but there's no excuse for anyone to work harder than you do."

Hunger is what drives us, what keeps us going even when it hurts. Hunger is that desire to be your absolute best self, no matter what it takes. In short, if our daughters and sons are going to achieve greatness, *they gotta want it*! We often see hunger for growth spring up in our children early, after they have some initial success. But this does not mean that that hunger will be long-lasting.

I am a firm believer that you cannot achieve something until you believe that thing is possible. And the best way to foster belief—and the hunger that comes from it—is by seeing that thing with your own eyes.

When my daughters were young, I would introduce them to athletes that were further along than them to give them an opportunity to see what greatness looked like, to witness what a deep drive could bring about. We would often attend the local high school games together and talk about how exciting it would be when they were playing on the team one day. I would spend time watching the sports they wanted to watch and made a point to watch women's sports (parents of girls, take note). In all of this, I wanted to give them a vision for their lives and future. I wanted to give them fuel for their dreams and the hunger they would need.

I encouraged them that they too could find that kind of greatness if they went at it with an insatiable hunger. I taught them that greatness was not reserved for a select few born with the right abilities, but that they too could have greatness in their future. I wanted them to imagine themselves in those places, taking those shots, knowing in their hearts that they could accomplish truly remarkable things. This is because I knew that before they could achieve something so difficult, they first had to believe it to be possible.

All that is left then is setting them free in mouthwatering pursuit of that which they know they can have. To go and get their dream with an uncommon and tireless belief that they can achieve true greatness.

Like I said before, hunger is hard to teach, but we as parents can nudge them, encourage them, and help them to refocus on what they dream. We can awaken hunger in them by helping them to see positive examples of it and believe it is possible also for them. And when true hunger is awakened, it will help them to push through even the most difficult of challenges on the way to their dream.

HUMILITY IS UNDERVALUED

This final pathway to greatness is one that I often find people underestimating the power of. That is what makes the following statement so vital despite what culture would have us believe.

Without humility true success cannot be achieved.

Go back and read that again for good measure. We often think of humility as highlighting our deficiencies and putting ourselves down for the sake of quashing our pride. I want to suggest another definition, however.

Humility is to have an accurate and grounded understanding of yourself, with both your limitations and capabilities.

That means humility is understanding the truth about yourself. Its antitheses, then, are both arrogance and insecurity—which many of us know are two sides to the same coin. Both arrogance and insecurity attack us at the level of our identity. Insecurity says that because of our limitations, we have less value. And when we believe we have less value, it is difficult for us to visualize success for ourselves. Arrogance, on the other hand, tries to convince us that our achievements, skills, and talents are what gives us value. We then spend our time trying to prove our value to ourselves and others through achievement and boasting.

Where insecurity and arrogance stifle our growth, humility makes us stronger. It helps us to see ourselves and everyone else rightly, as people of inherent value who have limitations but are capable of greatness. When we have a good sense of our inherent value as human beings, we are unleashed from the torment of continuously working to earn it. The process of growth is then simply becoming more yourself.

Some of my favorite athletes to watch are those of great humility. They never see themselves as arrived and so they continue to get better. They feel no need to tear others down because they are completely secure in themselves.

You may be saying to yourself, "But Greg, some of the greatest athletes struggle with arrogance!" That may be true, but I believe you will find that, though their humility may not transfer to the rest of their lives, most great athletes hold a healthy level of humility when it comes to their craft. They understand their limits and shortcomings so that they can work on them. They know when to ask for help and when to rely on others.

On the other side of humility, they understand that greatness is within reach of those who are willing to work for it. They know that they can hit that shot, make that time, nail that routine. And therein lies the secret. The great Michael Jordan put it best when he said, "You must expect great things of yourself before you can do them."

Now, that said, I believe it is a huge loss to allow our humility to end with sports. Humility will serve our children in all areas of life.

Everybody likes to be around a humble person, because they know that person not only sees themself as having tremendous value, but sees and calls out the value in others. They understand their limits and give others space to have theirs. They are grounded in reality, while at the same time not selling themselves short. Humble people are lifelong learners and understand that they will always be works in progress. Humble people are happy to sacrifice for others and celebrate their teammates' successes.

Humble people are leaders, and we cannot underestimate how these kinds of leaders can bring greatness not just for themselves but for their families, schools, cities, states, countries, and world.

CHAPTER 4

BUILDING DISCIPLINE

Building a life of discipline is a necessity if your daughter or son is to succeed as an athlete. Furthermore, a life of discipline will serve your child far beyond sports and help them to operate with excellence in whatever they set out to do.

Our culture has a complicated relationship with discipline. Often associated with punishment, we think of discipline as something to be feared. I want to help you and your child instead see discipline as a friend, one that will serve them in the pursuit of their greatest dreams.

Internal *discipline* is a purposeful rhythm of life fostered over time for the sake of mastering a specific endeavor. Let's break that down into bite-size chunks.

First, discipline is *a purposeful rhythm of life*. Discipline is more than just dedication or perseverance—though it involves both. It is about having an intentional and well thought-out structure to your life on every level—daily, weekly, monthly, and beyond. It is a rhythm in the sense that it is a repeated pattern a person chooses for their life to follow.

For your kid, this means creating a balanced rhythm in their week (making sure they have thought through their schedule— when they will work out, do homework, rest, spend time with family, etc.). But it also means creating a balanced rhythm on a smaller scale (for example, a rhythm for each workout, a rhythm in the way they approach their studies, and so on). When practiced in this way, discipline is not following thoughtless rules, but rather living in a balanced, thoughtful, and healthy manner.

Next, discipline is *fostered over time.* Having discipline is not something that you can simply wish for and then instantly have. It is a muscle that you build through intentional work and over the course of time. It is true that discipline comes more naturally with practice. But we cannot expect our children to start there.

Finally, discipline is *for the sake of mastering a specific endeavor.* We are not asking our daughters and sons to pursue discipline for discipline's sake. Yes, internal discipline can (and should) be used as a general tool to better one's life. But I will mainly be talking about how discipline can be used specifically to advance your child's sports journey.

I hope to help you as a parent guide your daughters and sons as they learn to manage every aspect of their sports journey with excellence. By fostering a life of discipline, they will be able to do what is necessary to achieve a high level of success in sports and life.

TEACHING SELF-DISCIPLINE

Monica is a fourth grader who has a growing passion for softball. Monica's mom, Debbie, played in high school as a pitcher and Monica wants to start learning this very unique part of the game. They start a routine of going to the park to practice the basic form, footwork, grip, and release necessary to grow as a pitcher. In the beginning, Debbie is with Monica the entire time as she is practicing, gently encouraging and correcting Monica as she tries to build the necessary muscle memory.

After a couple months, Debbie buys a bucket of old softballs from a local batting cage and tapes a strike zone on a brick wall in the backyard. She has Monica set up a pitching mound the proper distance from the wall for continued practice. Debbie gets Monica started with her routine and then goes inside to let Monica practice on her own, checking on her occasionally to give encouragement and offer small corrections.

Monica is excited because of the progress she is seeing in her pitching and practices four to five times a week. Soon Monica is starting her pitching workout before Debbie is even home from work and even amending her routine to work on different pitches she has learned online. Debbie still collects balls for her on occasion but is impressed with Monica's personal dedication to the craft.

As parents, we know we have had success in instilling discipline in our children when we no longer need to tell our kids what is needed. Debbie started by patiently guiding Monica in a very hands-on way. In this, she encouraged and sharpened Monica's skills until she was ready to practice on her own. Slowly she backed off, giving Monica space to build in herself the discipline she was learning from her mom. Eventually Monica was not only working out on her own, but also showing initiative by finding amendments to her workout online.

This is an example of how you as a parent can teach your child to be *self*-disciplined.

A lot of athletes depend on someone always being there to teach or coach them. The best athletes, however, learn to work on their game on their own. This means your child has to be absolutely passionate about what they are doing. They will have to push themselves, while no one else is around, beyond their own comfort zone in order to grow.

As a wise athlete once said, "What you do when nobody is watching is what separates a champion from everybody else."[16]

Teaching discipline is like setting up scaffolding for your child. In the beginning, they will need more of your help structuring their life inside and outside of sports. Our daughters and sons need us to model and encourage healthy rhythms as they learn how to live a disciplined life alongside us. As they grow, we gradually remove the scaffolding of our oversight, trusting them with a little bit more at a time. This helps children to build internal strength while still having us available to nudge and encourage them along the way.

This subtle method of teaching discipline is supportive while simultaneously nonintrusive. It teaches our kids that they can be trusted to manage their own athletic journeys (and lives) with increasing responsibility, all while they are in the safety of a loving family with parents who will help them when needed. It is the athletes that are able to work on their craft when no one else is watching—not you, not a coach, not a trainer—who are able to achieve the greatest heights. The ones who have learned

---

16 Source unknown.

to have discipline in and of themselves are able to self-initiate, self-motivate, and self-correct, even at a young age.

Now this doesn't mean they won't need your guidance and support. Giving your child room to grow should never make them feel like they are in it alone. Even today, I go with my adult daughters to work out, mostly just to rebound and spend time together. Occasionally they will ask my advice or need me to be a sounding board for them, but it is *their* journey that I have the privilege of witnessing and being welcomed into.

Remember though, this sort of discipline did not just appear in my daughters overnight. When my girls were young, we found the best place to teach discipline was in our home. Teaching discipline at home carries over back to sports and the rest of life. Their mother and I would start by doing little tasks with them. One of us would make the bed with them, tidy up their room as a team, help them get ready for school with our support, and things like that. Eventually, we would ask them to do these tasks on their own and check in every so often to see if they needed help (little ones often do). Soon, I would find I did not need to ask and they were starting to master the tasks we had given them.

By the time they were in the second or third grade, they were setting their own alarm, getting themselves ready for school, and even making their own lunches the night before. In their athletic journeys, they themselves made sure that they were ready for practice or a game by getting their own equipment ready, grabbing their own water or sports drink from the cupboard, and making sure we as parents got them there on time. They learned to initiate their personal workouts and eventually guide those themselves, though they often liked having me there with them.

Yes, their mother and I had to often step in to correct and encourage, but the more room we trusted them with, the more they learned that they were *able*. Able to succeed. Able to grow into the kind of person that can make wild dreams a reality.

DISCIPLINE GROWS FROM A BALANCED SCHEDULE

Athletes often have long days filled with school, practice, individual workouts, and homework, all while trying to fit in time for family, friends, and hopefully to get some rest. Without intentional and well thought-out scheduling, an athlete can burn out quickly.

This is why I recommend you help your child grow in self-discipline by teaching them to take responsibility for their own weekly schedule at an early age. This will help your daughter or son learn to be responsible with their time and accountable for their commitments.

For younger children, I recommend starting small by buying a paper calendar to hang on your child's bedroom wall. When they are little, you are simply teaching them to read the calendar and keep track of the date. As they grow in understanding, you want to help them to start writing activities and marking important dates on the calendar. By the time they are in middle school, you should be encouraging them to keep track of their own homework, tests, practices, games, and other activities. Once they have these set times recorded, help them to think through how they want to intentionally schedule the rest of their time.

It might be helpful at first to sit with your sixth or seventh grader each week and help them plan out the next seven days. This mostly looks like asking them helpful questions that get them in the habit of thinking through their week. *When are you planning on doing homework? Do you have a test this week you need to make time to study for? When do you want to do your individual workouts this week?*[17]

And most importantly, *How can I help you this week?*

This last question helps them to know that you are there for them, while at the same time giving them the responsibility to invite you into their week on their terms.

Also take time to be interested in how things are going by checking in on your daughter or son. *How are things going with your week? Are you feeling overwhelmed? What adjustments do you think we can make? Is there something unanticipated that you realize you need my help with?* No need to hit them with this barrage all at once, but pepper these questions in throughout the week. This will help you to build an open line of communication so that they know they can turn to you for help.

THE IMMENSE IMPORTANCE OF REST

This section may feel ironic coming on the heels of our last section. You may yourself feel a bit overwhelmed with all your child will have to juggle as an athlete.

Pause for a second. Take a deep breath.

---

17 **Side Note:** This will really help you as a parent as well. Remember, you're still their Uber driver.

I intentionally put this section on rest here to highlight its importance to a disciplined life. It is well-known that we as human beings need rest. And if your young athlete wants to succeed at the highest level, it will be good for them to make rest a priority.

Let's start with *Rest 101*: your daily sleep pattern. Children who get the recommended hours of sleep on a consistent basis are sharper, healthier, and happier. Without consistency in their sleep schedule, it's unlikely that your daughter or son will ever truly feel rested. Furthermore, sleep deprivation can stunt a child's physical and mental development,[18] and it can even heighten their risk of mental health problems such as anxiety and depression.[19]

What's worse, according to an article in the journal *Sports Medicine*, "athletes may experience a reduced quality and/or quantity of sleep."[20] The article goes on to say that, "Sleep deprivation can have significant effects on athletic performance, especially submaximal, prolonged exercise. Compromised sleep may also influence learning, memory, cognition, pain perception, immunity and inflammation."[21]

It is clear why a disciplined sleep rhythm is such a big deal for the best athletes. LeBron James—NBA veteran for near two

18 Leila Tarokh, Jared M. Saletin, Mary A. Carskadon, "Sleep in adolescence: Physiology, cognition and mental health," *Neuroscience & Biobehavioral* Reviews (epub August 13, 2016): https://pubmed.ncbi.nlm.nih.gov/27531236/.

19 Massimiliano de Zambotti, Aimee Goldstone, Ian M Colrain, Fiona C. Baker, "Insomnia disorder in adolescence: Diagnosis, impact, and treatment," *Sleep Medicine* Reviews (epub July 1, 2017): https://pubmed.ncbi.nlm.nih.gov/28974427/.

20 Halson, S.L., "Sleep in Elite Athletes and Nutritional Interventions to Enhance Sleep," *Sports Med* 44 (2014): 13–23, https://doi.org/10.1007/s40279-014-0147-0.

21 Halson, S.L., "Sleep in Elite Athletes and Nutritional Interventions to Enhance Sleep," *Sports Med* 44 (2014): 13–23, https://doi.org/10.1007/s40279-014-0147-0.

decades, four-time champion, four-time MVP, and future hall-of-famer—has been known to highlight sleep as one of his main keys to success. He strives for eight-to-ten hours of sleep a night, plus naps throughout the day.[22]

Of course, this kind of sleep will not always be possible for your child, but striving for consistency in this area will help them in virtually every aspect of life.

I also recommend consistent rest in your child's week. On most non-game days your child should be engaging in some sort of individual workout, but this does not have to be extensive every day. Even forty-five minutes to an hour on some days can make a huge difference. And they definitely should not be pushing each workout beyond two hours.

As far as games, it is not healthy for your young athlete to be playing more than two games in a day. This is an issue with many AAU and select-team sports. As parents, we need to protect our kids from this sort of overworking.

I suggest, before your daughter or son commits to a team, having a conversation with the coach. Respectful, honest communication is a cornerstone of all healthy relationships, and your relationship with your child's coach is no different. Ask them what sort of time commitment is involved, and lay out for them a realistic expectation for how much your child will play in a given day. I personally had this conversation with my daughter's AAU coach, who was very receptive.

---

22 *The Tim Ferriss Show*, "LeBron James and his Top-Secret Trainer, Mike Mancias," no. 349.

Coaches, if you are reading this, it is not fair to ask a player to play three or four games in a day. A child's body is not equipped to handle that level of intensity all day long, weekend after weekend. We have to keep in mind the best interest of each of the players entrusted into our care.

It is also an immensely helpful practice for an athlete to take one day off a week from athletics (both physically and mentally). This practice has been shown over and over again to have tremendous benefits in longevity, injury prevention, and stamina. Ideally your child would be able to take a full twenty-four-hour period off per week to rest from sports and school.

If twenty-four hours isn't possible, what would it look like to help them set aside eighteen or sixteen hours to get away from their training and schoolwork, and just rest their body and mind? I've found this practice is also good for families to do together. Not that you have to be in the same room the whole time, but let's model a healthy lifestyle for our children and reap the benefits ourselves also.

Lastly, there are numerous benefits for athletes in taking consistent yearly rest, away from sports, at the end of each season. Many successful athletes play sports "year-round." Even single-sport athletes at the highest level are playing both for school and select teams. This makes finding time to step away from sports difficult.

This is exactly why it is vital that you help them carve out six weeks, twice a year, to put down sports and just be a kid.

I have to be up-front with you: this will not just happen. Busyness is like a goldfish: it will fill the container you give it. And the world of youth sports is no different. There will always be another season, another tournament, and another workout initiative that will be demanding your daughter's or son's time. One of the best things you can teach your kids is when to say *no*.

Sports seasons will cause them to miss birthday parties, dances, school activities, and at times, holidays. This sacrifice is one of the most difficult parts of being an athlete *and* a parent of an athlete.

When my daughters were in high school and playing varsity basketball—for four years, while living in Portland, Oregon—I couldn't visit my family in Ohio over Christmas because of a reoccurring holiday tournament. That was tough, but it was a sacrifice I was willing to make for my daughters.

The six weeks after the season, however, is an opportunity to reverse that trend and make the other stuff a priority. It is a time for your kid to be with friends, doing things that they enjoy outside of sports. It's a time for supporting family (parents and siblings) in the activities and interests they are involved in.

It's time to give the body and mind a break from the constant pressure a sports season can bring. (If they want, they can do a few light workouts a week that are not related to their primary sport.) It makes the most sense for them to take this time immediately after the season. That way they can slowly work back into shape after they have taken their six weeks, in preparation for the start of the next season.

Take time off yourself in this period to get extra, undistracted time with your children. According to a study in *Harvard Business Review*:

People who took fewer than 10 of their vacation days per year had a 34.6% likelihood of receiving a raise or bonus in a three-year period of time. People who took more than 10 of their vacation days had a 65.4% chance of receiving a raise or bonus. If you take 11 or more of your vacation days, you are more than 30% more likely to receive a raise.[23]

So go get your raise and your own rest. If you can pull it off, consider a family getaway. Even something inexpensive like going camping for a few days can be a unifying experience for your family.

CHARACTER: A DEEPER DISCIPLINE

Instilling athletic discipline in your child is important, but it is near meaningless if you do not leverage that into a discipline of morality. Moral discipline, or ***character***, is a rhythm, built over time and repeated action, of doing what is right in every arena of life. Though high character is incredibly beneficial to those who possess it, we pursue high character with others in mind.

Similar to all forms of discipline, the fruit of character is best identified when no one is watching. John Wooden once said, "Be more concerned with your character than your reputation. Because your character is what you really are, while your reputation is merely what others think you are." Character is instilled in our children to the degree that they do what is right, respectful,

---

23 Shawn Achor and Michelle Gielan, "The Data-Driven Case for Vacation," *Harvard Business Review* (July 13, 2016): https://hbr.org/2016/07/the-data-driven-case-for-vacation.

selfless, kind, courageous, and virtuous when we are not around to tell them to. And as our kids get older, the stakes get higher. They go from choices about being kind on the schoolyard to making decisions about drugs, sex, and alcohol.

I have been blessed with daughters of high character. Some of it was their mother's and my intentional way of raising them, and some of it is by the grace of God. This will be true for all of our kids. But shame on us if we do not do all we can to put our daughters and sons in the best possible position to grow into people of high character. This is one of those *bigger than sports* things that will assist your daughters and sons in every aspect of their lives. Though sports, again, provides us a tremendous opportunity as parents to instill deeper values into the lives of our kids.

Teaching character in sports—as we have already discussed in chapter two—starts with teaching our children to have respect for every aspect of the game and each person involved. Respect for the game means not trying to take a shortcut, and knowing that every choice has a consequence (positive, negative, or otherwise). Respect for each person means treating teammates, coaches, referees, opponents, parents, teachers, and all others with the dignity they deserve as human beings.

Character is subtle, taught over time in a million little moments in a million different ways.

This, first and foremost, will come through what we personally model for our children as their parents. The *do as I say, not as I do* mantra is not actually all that helpful. If we are constantly yelling at refs or coaches, that is communicating that respect and kindness towards others is not as important as expressing our own anger. If we lack integrity because we do not follow through with what we say we will do, then our kids will not have a high value for following through.

Character is also shaped by the coaches, mentors, and friends that are within our kids' close orbit. It is important for us as parents to be deliberate about those we let teach and influence our kids. It is also key that we teach them to seek out friends with similar values and high character. Not that they should be judgmental of others, but that they are thoughtful about who they invest their time with.

All that said, none of this is a perfect science and it is good for us to continuously be assessing, correcting course, and then reassessing. There is no sure thing when it comes to raising kids, but I believe that if you are intentional about instilling discipline and character in your child, they will be formed in a way that helps them to succeed in sports, and in life beyond.

DISCIPLINED SCHEDULE WORKSHEET

Have your daughter or son re-create the worksheet on the opposite page in a planner or separate notebook.

1.   *Insert all the non-flexible parts of your weekly schedule first (school, practice, church, sleep, etc.).*

2.   *Next, have them schedule in things that have to be done, but don't have to be performed at a specific time. Have them start with the most important things and work their way down to the least important (e.g., 1. family time, 2. homework, 3. individual workouts, 4. time with friends, and so on).*

3.   *Finally, they can take the rest of their time and schedule things that they would like to do but that are not absolutely necessary.*

WEEKLY SCHEDULE:

MON	TUES	WED	THURS	FRI	SAT	SUN
5-6:00a	5-6:00a	5-6:00a	5-6:00a	5-6:00a	5-6:00a	5-6:00a
6-7:00a	6-7:00a	6-7:00a	6-7:00a	6-7:00a	6-7:00a	6-7:00a
7-8:00a	7-8:00a	7-8:00a	7-8:00a	7-8:00a	7-8:00a	7-8:00a
8-9:00a	8-9:00a	8-9:00a	8-9:00a	8-9:00a	8-9:00a	8-9:00a
9-10:00a	9-10:00a	9-10:00a	9-10:00a	9-10:00a	9-10:00a	9-10:00a
10-11:00a	10-11:00a	10-11:00a	10-11:00a	10-11:00a	10-11:00a	10-11:00a
11-12:00p	11-12:00p	11-12:00p	11-12:00p	11-12:00p	11-12:00p	11-12:00p
12-1:00p	12-1:00p	12-1:00p	12-1:00p	12-1:00p	12-1:00p	12-1:00p
1-2:00p	1-2:00p	1-2:00p	1-2:00p	1-2:00p	1-2:00p	1-2:00p
2-3:00p	2-3:00p	2-3:00p	2-3:00p	2-3:00p	2-3:00p	2-3:00p
3-4:00p	3-4:00p	3-4:00p	3-4:00p	3-4:00p	3-4:00p	3-4:00p
4-5:00p	4-5:00p	4-5:00p	4-5:00p	4-5:00p	4-5:00p	4-5:00p
5-6:00p	5-6:00p	5-6:00p	5-6:00p	5-6:00p	5-6:00p	5-6:00p
6-7:00p	6-7:00p	6-7:00p	6-7:00p	6-7:00p	6-7:00p	6-7:00p
7-8:00p	7-8:00p	7-8:00p	7-8:00p	7-8:00p	7-8:00p	7-8:00p
8-9:00p	8-9:00p	8-9:00p	8-9:00p	8-9:00p	8-9:00p	8-9:00p
9-10:00p	9-10:00p	9-10:00p	9-10:00p	9-10:00p	9-10:00p	9-10:00p

CHAPTER 5

UNDERSTANDING YOUR CHILD'S DEVELOPMENT

As we begin this chapter, I want to preface it by saying that each athlete's development is unique. Thus, we cannot definitively break stages of development down by age. Some will grow more quickly and others will be late bloomers. What you will find in this chapter are generalities about these age groups and what I have found most effective and appropriate for these age groups in my decades of experience.

It is important, though, that you as a parent are in tune with your child's unique development and support them accordingly. You have the chance to know your child better than anyone else and can help them to work on what is appropriate for their level of development.

Take Anthony for example:

As a fourth grader, Anthony shows a ton of promise as a basketball player. Despite being smaller than most children his age, his quickness and above-average hand-eye coordination make him stand out from his peers. His mom, who played basketball collegiately, has been trying to help Anthony improve the form of his shot. Because Anthony is so small, he has trouble shooting the ball above his head. Instead, he flings it from his waist.

Anthony's mom understands that developmentally this makes sense. Both she and Anthony's dad were late bloomers and did not gain much size until high school. She just has Anthony work on proper form closer to the basket while in practice, trusting that her son's arm strength will increase as he matures.

By the time he is in middle school, his form is perfect on his midrange shots and he is able to shoot from chest height from longer distances. She knows that if he keeps increasing his range each year as he grows in strength, he will be able to shoot with perfect form from all over the court by the time his growth spurt hits in the next couple years.

Anthony's mom knows her son, when he will likely grow, and how to help him develop slowly at the pace that makes the most sense for him. She is not overly concerned with comparison and is simply helping her son focus on the fundamentals and on learning to work hard. This is a perfect example of developmental understanding and patience.

As you go through this chapter, keep your daughter or son and their unique development in mind. Also, remember no scholarships are given at this level. It's truly a process.

ELEMENTARY SCHOOL: HEALTH, HABITS, AND FUNDAMENTALS

When our daughters and sons are in elementary school, our goal is not primarily about their growth in a particular sport. Now don't hear me wrong: if your daughter or son approaches elementary-level athletics properly, they will get better, but this isn't what we should be primarily concerned with at this point.

Elementary athletics is primarily about teaching your kid *how to go about* working on whatever athletic craft is before them.

Remember they are, at this point, still discovering their love of sports. This means we are encouraging in them a well-rounded and diverse athletic experience involving a number of different sports and roles within those sports. Pushing them to be hyper-focused on a single sport or specialization within a particular sport is premature.

Not only so, but it can also harm their physical development. A fascinating study in the *American Journal of Sports Medicine* suggests that multisport participation at the youth level has a direct correlation to injury prediction among NBA players. The study found that out of the 237 professional athletes included in the study,

36 (15%) were multisport athletes and 201 (85%) were single-sport athletes in high school. The multisport cohort played in a statistically significantly greater percentage of total games (78.4% vs 72.8%; P < .001). Participants in the multisport cohort were less likely to sustain a major injury during their career (25% vs 43%, P = .03). Finally, a greater percentage of the multisport athletes were active in the league at time of data acquisition, indicating increased longevity in the NBA (94% vs 81.1%; P = .03).[24]

24 Caitlin Rugg et al., "The Effects of Playing Multiple High School Sports on National Basketball Association Players' Propensity for Injury and Athletic Performance," *The American Journal of Sports Medicine* (November 14, 2017): https://doi.org/https://doi.org/10.1177/0363546517738736.

Those are some staggering numbers when you think about it. Though the research was inconclusive as to why such a relation exists, one possibility is the increase of risk for muscle imbalance.

Muscle imbalance occurs when one muscle or group of muscles become stronger than others as a result of overuse. It is well-known that such imbalance is a huge factor as far as injury is concerned. Single-sport athletes are far more likely to focus their training solely around the musculoskeletal groups that their sport of choice involves.

If a young athlete continues this pattern at a high-intensity level sustained over much of their childhood, they are at a high risk of muscle imbalance and injury.

You may have noticed that the study involved professionals that were multisport athletes in *high school*. How much more are we putting our children at risk if we allow them to be single-sport athletes as seven-year-olds? This multisport strategy of course must be paired with healthy rhythms of rest and body care as discussed prior, but the research is clear.

It is far more beneficial to encourage multisport athletics for our daughters and sons *for as long as possible*.

That is why this elementary stage of your child's athletic development is focused more on how they go about working on their craft than it is on anything else. Most of what we are discussing in this section about elementary-age athletes is written with third through sixth graders in mind. Of course, you can and should encourage your younger children to play sports, have fun, be active, and learn healthy, age-appropriate discipline, but in my experience the more serious work begins from the third grade on.

The three emphases of this stage are as follows:

- **Healthy Living:** First, we want to model and help our children develop healthy and balanced physical care. This means teaching healthy approaches to exercise, rest, nutrition, and even aspects of health beyond what is physical. This is the strong foundation on which you want your daughter or son to build their sports journey. This doesn't mean no fun, though! I occasionally make room for one of my favorites: ice cream!

- **Habit Building:** Next is helping them to build habits around their athletic pursuits that will lead them to success. A lot of this goes back to the building of discipline. Help them to take the discipline they are learning at home and apply it to their athletic journey. It is all about incorporating a balanced routine into all they do—study habits, sleeping habits, workout habits, and so on.

- **The Fundamentals:** Finally, with elementary-age athletes, a focus on the fundamentals of each sport they participate in is key. Building a basic understanding and skill set for a sport is something that an athlete comes back to again and again throughout their sports journey.

Let's first talk about helping our children build a healthy lifestyle. This does not mean that we have to turn our kids into over-the-top health nuts. What it does mean is that it is important for our children's futures that we prioritize in our homes healthy eating habits, regular exercise, and a balanced schedule of rest. This is one of those things that are *caught* better than *taught*.

If health is a priority for us as parents, then there is a good chance it will be a priority for our daughters and sons.

We will talk more about many of these aspects of a healthy lifestyle in the chapters to come, but I do want to take a moment and highlight some non-physical aspects of a healthy life—though many of these will have physical impact on you and your children.

Primarily, I'd like to highlight the importance of healthy boundaries, especially for athletes at the elementary level. Though I do think it's good for serious elementary-age athletes to take time for their personal athletic development four to five times a week, we cannot force this type of regimen on our kids. We can help them to understand that this is the way serious athletes train, but it is also okay for them to just want to have fun.

This is teaching them to have healthy boundaries, even with you. They are their own person and, to a certain degree, should be able to make choices about their sports journey—as long as those choices are healthy for them.

I also think part of teaching healthy boundaries at this age is monitoring and guarding their time—and subsequently your own. This is why I encourage athletes in this age group to stay local (within your city or county) when it comes to their athletics. Some in youth sports will encourage nationwide travel for your third through seventh grader, year-round competition in a single sport, and three or four tournaments a month. This is excessive, unhealthy, and unnecessary.

These sorts of demands can become quite exhausting to the athlete, parents, and siblings. Instead, use this time to invest in your family and yourself. It is so much easier to instill healthy boundaries and prioritize family at this age than it is when our children are older, and this will serve our daughters and sons' mental health throughout their lives. (Coaches, it is important we also understand this and partner with parents in this endeavor.)

Sure, your daughter or son may want to play in one or two tournaments a year, somewhere in your larger region. But, overall, the time and money that this will take from you is not worth it at the elementary level.

Further, part of building healthy boundaries is helping your young child to understand what appropriate and inappropriate relationships look like with adults other than you. Yes, this means teaching them about respect, being coachable, and listening well, but it also involves training them to identify red flags and when healthy boundaries are being crossed by an adult or person in power.

Not only that, we need to come up with a plan for how to handle such worrisome behavior from coaches, assistants, aides, and even other parents in the event it occurs. This is where safe adults need to be in lockstep with one another in teaching our children to live with their eyes open.

When it comes to elementary-age kids, I would recommend wise practices such as: watching practices and games rather than just dropping your child off, not allowing your daughter or son to be alone with an adult that is not a part of their family, and not allowing digital correspondence (texting, social media, phone calls, online gaming, etc.) directly to your child from an adult who is not a part of their family. These sorts of boundaries are good to keep in place even through middle school and, in some cases, high school.

We as parents have a responsibility to protect our kids, and it is better to approach these types of things with an abundance of caution.

The next emphasis of elementary-age athletes is habit building around sports. If we are already helping them to build this sort of discipline at home, then transferring discipline over to their athletic journey is somewhat natural.

Remembering our definition of discipline—a purposeful rhythm of life fostered over time for the sake of mastering a specific endeavor—we are simply helping them to build personal habits in keeping with their sports goals.

If they do choose the life of a serious athlete at this stage of development, part of habit building is teaching them to work on their craft. This most likely means individual workouts four to five times a week, with no more than ninety minutes a session. Some of you may be thinking that this is a lot, but keep in mind that you are helping them simply to get in the habit of taking athletics seriously.

We are teaching them how to work hard, practice consistently and effectively, and enjoy the process. Help them to set goals for each workout (e.g., a certain amount of makes, miles, serves, etc.). You don't need to have crazy-high expectations when they are young, but as they grow, help them to increase reps each year.

Habits are hard to start, but they are also hard to break.

The last emphasis of elementary-age athletics is learning and practicing the fundamentals of each sport that is pursued. If there is a particular sport that you do not understand, do some research online, talk to some local coaches, and ask them what your kid should be working on at this point. Watch the sport with your child and help them understand everything that is going on. If kids do not understand the fundamentals of a particular sport, they have little chance of being a successful athlete long-term.

This doesn't mean that kids cannot have fun trying the wild moves they see the pros do and dreaming of creative and jaw-dropping plays. When I was a kid, I was Magic Johnson, throwing wild passes behind my back to my teammate cutting to the basket. After all, at the end of the day, sports are meant to be fun, and far be it from me to stifle that sort of creativity.

All of those dazzling moves, though—the bicycle kicks, ankle-breaking crossovers, glove flips to second base—are built on the fundamentals. Help your kids to see the importance of the basics and build to the creative stuff from there.

MIDDLE SCHOOL: RESPONSIBILITY, ACCOUNTABILITY, AND FUNDAMENTALS (AGAIN)

Our emphases for the middle school stage of development are:

- **Take Responsibility:** You want to start to help your daughter or son take charge of their own athletic journey. You are still very much with them in it, but you want them to be the initiator and the driving force of their sports journey.

- **Embrace Accountability:** As we encourage increasing levels of responsibility, we also want to help our children embrace accountability. At the end of the day, they are the ones who have to answer for their time.

- **Sharpen the Fundamentals:** Yes, fundamentals are still key at the middle school stage. Hopefully they can sharpen them as they go through early maturing and start to gain greater strength and coordination.

So let's start with responsibility. As your daughter or son moves into the seventh and eighth grade, it is time to teach them to take responsibility for their own athletic development and balance of schedule.

Help them to see that, though you are always there for them, if they truly want to succeed as an athlete, they will have to learn to manage and motivate themselves. Communicate to them that they can be trusted, that the patterns that you have modeled and taught them will serve them well. Also, communicate that with greater trust comes greater accountability. They will have to answer to you, their coaches, and their teammates for how they are approaching their increasing freedom.

And when trust is abused, do not meet their mistakes with distance or isolation. Rather, it is our job as parents to bring our kids close again to help guide them back to paths of health and success. This isn't something that happens all at once, and our children will need grace as they navigate leaving behind childhood to become responsible teenagers.

With increased responsibility and accountability comes increased activity. Successful athletes at the middle school level should be increasing their individual workouts to six times a week, an hour and a half a session. And in these sessions, they will want their goals and expectations of themselves to increase (e.g., higher percentage of makes, moving at game speed, working to beat a specific time, etc.). I would not recommend weight training at this point, but it can be helpful to introduce band and bodyweight exercises (push-ups, sit-ups, pull-ups, etc.).

In these workouts, they are now starting to refine their fundamentals, learning to focus on skill development (something we will explore more in depth in the next chapter). At this point they may want to begin focusing on two main sports and the skills surrounding those sports.

I think it is also appropriate at this point to expand their athletic endeavors beyond the local level and start exploring more state and regional competitions. We are not talking all the time, but two to three tournaments in the region per season, with perhaps one competition on a more national level, can be a fun and worthwhile growing experience for your kid. (This, of course, is all in the context of you going with them.)

It's also important for your daughter or son to start noticing college coaches at these events. Recognizing a coach they have seen on TV in the gym watching local talent can continue to propel their dream of playing at their favorite college.

I still advise against the three to four tournaments a month that some athletes this age are accustomed to. That is just too much and does not leave enough time for rest, family, and for your child to grow socially and have a life outside of sports. Talk with coaches beforehand to get a good sense of the demand that a particular team makes and decide if it is compatible with your values as a family.

Middle school may also be a good time to consider hiring a trainer who can assist your child in preparing for the next level. I do not recommend relying on trainers however. We are trying to instill a sense of athletic responsibility in our children. Some athletes can become overdependent on trainers and coaches. It is important for them to understand that the real growth happens when no one is looking.

Furthermore, with select teams, increased travel, and trainers, things can get very expensive quickly. If money is tight, I encourage you to get creative. Ask about scholarship opportunities with select teams. Split travel costs with another family who is willing to carpool to far-off tournaments. Talk to a local coach or older successful player about discounted personal sessions. There are so many great coaches out there who coach for the right reason and are willing to help.

Also, remind your children that they have some of the best athletes and trainers in the world right at their fingertips—literally! Help your kids find drills online that the pros and their trainers use, so that they can set up their own training sessions at home. Offer to film your kid while they train so that they can compare their form to the videos they are finding online and make adjustments.

Have them take advantage of every possible resource through which to improve their game. This is what sets them apart when they enter the next level, high school.

HIGH SCHOOL: HARD WORK, SPECIALIZATION, AND (YOU GUESSED IT) FUNDAMENTALS

When I was in high school, I had a teammate named Billy Ward. Billy was not the most gifted athlete, but I always admired his work ethic. As a junior, Billy played on the JV team while many of his peers had already moved on to the varsity level.

Now there is no shame in this and I don't mean it as a criticism. We had a good high school team and the competition was fierce. But Billy decided that he wanted more out of his high school athletic experience as a senior.

In the off-season leading into our senior season, Billy lived in the gym. I thought I was serious about basketball, but when I arrived, Billy had already been there for an hour. And on my way out, the young man was still there, putting up shots. He had it in his mind that he would not only make the varsity team, but that he would be a starter.

By the time the season came around, Billy's shot was automatic. So much so that the local newspaper started calling him "Bingo" Billy Ward. Not only did he start on our team, he was named to the all-conference team, and even earned a college scholarship to Wittenberg University in Springfield, Ohio. To this day, I still think of all Billy was able to accomplish with determination and hard work.

I tell this story to underscore what high school sports are all about. Somewhere along the way many of us believed the lie that the primary component of success—especially in sports—is talent. Yes, some people are born with a leg up talentwise, but if I had to choose between the talented and the hardworking, it really isn't close.

Let's look at our emphases for the high school athlete (of which *hard work* is premiere):

- **Hard Work:** Yes, hard work needs to be a focus throughout their journey, but it takes special precedence for the high school athlete. They will need to learn that ultimately this is what will take them over the top.

- **Specialization:** Now is the time for your daughters and sons to start really honing their specialized skills for their sport and/or role. They should start paying special attention to what makes sense.

- **Back to the Basics (the Fundamentals):** And fundamentals again. This is all about teaching our kids to make the minor adjustments they need in order to overcome struggles by returning to the keys that helped them to improve in the first place.

For starters, high school is the developmental stage of your daughter's or son's athletic journey that is built primarily on hard work.

Your son or daughter may have a chance to play varsity as an underclassman. This is a huge shift coming straight from eighth-grade sports and into the varsity level. The game is faster, the athletes are stronger, the strategies more intellectual, the plays and signals more advanced. All that on top of adjusting to a new school and adapting to higher academic demands.

If they are to thrive—rather than just survive—as a student athlete at the high school level, they will have to be on top of their schedule from the time they get up to the time they go to bed. If they have eight hours to sleep and eight hours for school and practice, that leaves them another eight hours that they will have to be extremely wise with.[25] This will help them to be ready for the college level, where keeping a well-planned schedule is paramount to succeeding.

With a base built on discipline and health, and the head start they have in their skill development, they should be set up to really go to work as a high schooler. It will just take some transition and a bit more of your guidance.

This extends to both sports and academics. As we prepare our kids for college, we want them to develop good study habits and learn how to set up their own study hall sessions. The first year or two of high school, you are going to have to check work, as they will likely feel overwhelmed. But by sophomore or junior year they have usually gotten the hang of it.

On the athletic side, I often tell people that the difference between first place and last place in a sprint is tenths of a second. What will elevate an athlete above the competition will be their willingness to do what it takes to be great. It may just be the difference between making the team or not, starting or living

---

25 See the *Disciplined Schedule Worksheet* at the end of chapter four.

on the bench, getting that scholarship or walking away from the game after high school. We have to ask them this question, in some form: *Are you willing to put in the additional work to elevate yourself just that tiny bit more?*

That means extra time in individual workouts and in the weight room (now that they are in high school, it is good to introduce weight training into their routine). It means extra time studying film and learning the game.

This is also where specialization comes into play. Once in high school, you want to help your child identify the sport and/ or role their skill set best supports. I still think it is best to be a multisport athlete in high school—though I recognize this is not the way youth sports are going—but within each sport, where can your child work on their craft in order to best support their team?

Are they playing in the infield? Have them work on effectively stopping ground balls and throwing at multiple arm angles to various bases. Are they fighting to be the starting setter on their team? Have them working tirelessly on their form, ball placement, and communication.

This doesn't mean they work only on one area of their game. They should definitely continue to develop a well-rounded game. But it does mean that they should find a focus through which they can contribute at the highest level.

This also means that athletes need to be honest with themselves as to what they can truly offer and what best sets them up for potentially going to the collegiate level.

If your daughter is a five-foot-five basketball player and she does not have the ball-handling skills or shooting ability to play at the guard or wing position, it is not likely that she can succeed at the next level. Have her put in the work to become a shooting specialist or a ball-handling expert in order to set her up for success. Every team needs a great ball handler or a great shooter.

Perhaps your son is struggling to get his pitches' mph out of the low seventies. It may be time for him to consider a move to third base or outfield. These are hard conversations, but having them can often help a child get more out of their high school sports experience.

Finally, a main focus for the high school athlete is continually coming back to and working on advancing their fundamentals. I know this feels repetitive, but that is how important this point is. Even professional athletes come back to the fundamentals when struggling or in a slump.

While I worked with Tiger, his dad would often be able to help him identify issues in his game by going back to the basics and helping him see the ever-so-slight discrepancy in his putting stroke or swing. When your daughter or son hits difficulty, remind them again to return to what got them this far in the first place.

As we go into the next chapter on skill development, these fundamentals will be our main focus. They are an absolute key to athletic success.

CHAPTER 6

EMPHASIZING SKILL DEVELOPMENT

There is an epic scene about halfway through the classic film *The Karate Kid*. Daniel, a bullied teenager hoping to learn to defend himself, has been taken under the wing of a karate master, Mr. Miyagi. At this point in the movie, Daniel-san—as he is famously referred to by his teacher—is fed up with Miyagi and the so-called training he is undergoing.

As far as Daniel-san can tell, all he has learned to do are the chores around Mr. Miyagi's house—painting his fence, sanding his deck, waxing his cars. And, to top it off, the karate master is super particular about the way these chores are done, constantly correcting the way the teen is going about these seemingly menial tasks. Miyagi makes sure Daniel-san keeps his feet placed just so, his knees bent, his form proper, his eyes up and on his task, his breathing slow and controlled.

After a few days of this, Daniel-san loses all patience with the old man, declaring in a fit of frustration that he quits. Before Daniel-san can leave, Miyagi calls the young man back. "Show me sand the floor," the karate teacher patiently commands. The boy, with much reluctance, shows Miyagi a half-hearted version of the motion he used to sand the floor. Miyagi again patiently corrects Daniel-san's balance, form, footwork, and vision as he has him go through the repeated movements practiced in each chore.

At last, as Daniel-san is starting to understand the old-man's methods, Miyagi attempts to strike the teen in various ways. The once-frustrated boy is shocked to realize that he is able to block every attempted punch and kick with the various motions that his muscles have memorized through the repeated action of doing these chores. Miyagi has taught Daniel-san the fundamental skills of self-defense—what the rest of his training will be built on—all over the course of a few days. And, in the process, he has earned Daniel-san's unwavering trust.

Mr. Miyagi understood something about athletics that many of us overlook: it is through the relentless practice of individual skills that an athlete will truly succeed.

No matter what sport your daughter or son sets out to excel in, proper skill development is indispensable. ***Skill development*** refers to the intentional practice of an isolated skill integral to a particular sport. As a player develops aptitude in that particular skill, they can move on to more advanced practices, but it is unwise to skip over the basics, as they are what more advanced skills are based on.

Let me give you an example. In baseball the basic skills are throwing, catching, hitting, and fielding. It would make very little sense for me as an athlete to focus on advanced skills like turning a double play or executing a rundown, if I have not yet learned to throw.

Or take basketball instead: it makes no sense for me to be working on elaborate crossovers before I have even learned to dribble. This doesn't mean I have to be a master at dribbling before I can *start* practicing a crossover, but I should at least be able to dribble while moving, or my crossover practice will be useless.

This means an athlete needs to put in countless unapplauded hours to develop each skill necessary to play the game at a high level. If an athlete does not practice these skills—and eventually at game speed—they will have trouble succeeding in game situations. Start by helping your child work on simpler things, and then slowly introduce more complex situations that they may face in a game or competition.

As the old adage says, *you play like you practice.*

When I was privileged enough to work with Tiger, I would often get to play practice rounds of golf with him. I was amazed at how thorough the man was about his preparation. He was constantly setting up situations that he might face during a tournament and practicing every shot imaginable. And it was this tireless skill development that has led him to greatness for the last two and a half decades.

When teaching my daughters to shoot, we started with their feet set, at a realistic distance from the basket, with no one around them. As they got the hang of it, they started practicing shooting off the dribble and moving further and further from the basket. Next, I had them learning to shoot while I had a hand in their face from various spots on the floor. Finally, we practiced shooting at game speed with a defender guarding them, trying to recreate a game-like situation. This gave them the skills and confidence they needed come game time to let the ball fly.

Though this sort of skill work is important during the season, the off-season is where an athlete really gets better. Each off-season, help your daughter or son set a goal around improving a particular skill. Yes, they will want to work on their all-around game, but focusing on developing a specific skill that was a weakness for them the season before can bear tremendous fruit.

Not only will this help them to learn the game, but it will prepare them to fix any issues that arise during a season or anytime throughout their athletic journey. Slumps in sports are common. When your daughter or son is struggling, returning to these fundamental skills will help them to figure out the adjustments that need to be made.

THERE IS NO SUBSTITUTE FOR HARD WORK

My coach, Lefty Driesell, gave me a plaque when I stepped foot on campus at the University of Maryland that read:

The harder you work, the luckier you'll get.

The discipline and hard work you have been instilling in your child is key for this sort of skill development to really be helpful. Yes, hiring trainers can help your daughter or son develop their skills, but it is not a replacement for putting in the work on their own time. Unlike *The Karate Kid*, you cannot skip through this part using a five-minute training montage set to inspirational music.

Hard work is how you become better. Period.

Chris Paul, one of the most skilled players in the NBA, points out to young athletes that his confidence is rooted in his preparation. Knowing you can succeed—and then actually succeeding—can only come from practice.

This process cannot be shortcut or cheated. If you are not putting in the work, it is hard to improve. Working on your skills only two to three times a week is just not enough to see significant improvement. In the off-season an athlete should be engaged in skill training five to six days a week. No exception!

As your daughter or son works on developing the skills of their sport of choice, there are four areas that require great attention: balance, footwork, form, and vision. No matter what the sport, these areas are consistently most important and all athletes will need to come back to them time after time. This will be our focus for the rest of this chapter.

BALANCE

The first thing you learn in pretty much every sport is to find a place of balance.

Bend your knees. Stay on your toes. Shift your weight. Get low. Stay in control.

Sound familiar? All these are commands coaches use to instill the importance of balance at an early age. **Athletic balance** describes an athlete's ability to maintain an advantageous center of mass and body control during a given athletic task. Whether our daughters and sons are serving a tennis ball, playing offensive line, or leaping through the air to spike a volleyball, acting from a place of control and balance is key.

Healthy athletic balance allows multiple muscle groups to work synergistically on a task, utilizing leverage and center of mass to their advantage. Imagine the spring-loaded plunger of a pinball machine. When set properly, all the force of the compressed spring is transferred from the tip of the metal rod and into the ball. The spring is using all the energy at its disposal to accomplish this single task.

In sports, it is similar. For example, when shooting a jump shot in basketball, having your feet balanced underneath you properly allows you to use the force generated from your legs, core, *and* upper body as you release the ball. This allows your form to stay pure and focused on proper release. On the other hand, if you are off-balance as you jump, the force of your legs is actually working against the power of your release, forcing you to sacrifice form for the sake of power, which can set your jump shot askew.

The importance of balance is universal across the sports world. When considering common ongoing struggles athletes face, I find the issue is often—at least in part—to do with poor balance.

Many will point to strengthening the muscle group of one's core as the most essential element to maintaining athletic balance. Certainly this is a huge part of the issue, and I encourage athletes to be conscious of their core while training. But I find that even some professional athletes struggle with balance. This is not because they lack core strength, but because they lack focus.

They are not working regularly on staying balanced in their skill development, and thus their balance is compromised during athletic competition.

Being acutely aware of one's balance during skills training will help an athlete greatly. If an athlete is conscious of staying balanced while training, the muscle memory they develop will help them to stay balanced while competing.

When it comes to learning balance, the necessary actions aren't overly complicated. It is more about emphasizing it every day, in every skill. When your daughter or son is young, you will have to remind them of their balance, but eventually you will want to teach them to ask themselves the question, "Am I balanced?"

When I swing the bat, am I falling away from the ball? Are my feet sliding around during my golf swing? When I go up for a layup, am I taking off from and landing on a balanced center of gravity? Am I almost falling over when I kick the soccer ball?

Balance is the beginning of all skills training and it is something that athletes will want to check in on and come back to throughout their *entire* athletic careers.

FOOTWORK & FORM

Athletic footwork is the specific placement and movement patterns of an athlete's feet during athletic competition or training.

Experts across the board agree that proper footwork is a fundamental aspect to competing at an high level in most sports.[26]

---

26 Of course, there are many sports, such as water, wheelchair, and equestrian athletics, where "footwork" is not a chief concern. I would suggest, however, that foot placement or wheelchair positioning still plays an important role in getting better in these pursuits.

Hall of Fame college basketball coach Mike Krzyzewski is known for saying that "footwork is one of the primary prerequisites to becoming a great player." Tennis legend Roger Federer claims, "My game is a lot about footwork. If I move well, I play well." And NFL head coach and quarterback guru, Sean McVay, once said,

> With any player, especially at quarterback, I don't care if you're talking Tom Brady or Peyton Manning or Drew Brees: you want to make sure to continue to hammer down the fundamentals, and it all starts with your feet. Everything starts with footwork.

It is clear that what sets successful athletes apart is impeccable footwork.

Balance and footwork go hand in hand. Top athletes know how to use their footing to gain extra balance and leverage in any given situation in order to gain every little advantage possible over their opponents.

But it is not something that will just happen or can simply be picked up over time. Good footwork can only come through muscle memory—through hours and hours of working on your game. It is the result of practiced action repeated until it is habituated to the point that it feels like second nature.

When helping your daughter or son learn the fundamental skills of a sport, spend plenty of time emphasizing proper footwork. And as they grow, make sure they continually come back to their footwork, sharpening and shaping their skills as they go.

Footwork can easily become sloppy, especially when an athlete doesn't work on it regularly in their skills training. As a result, it is something the best professionals emphasize in their training even late into their careers.

Like footwork, proper form can make a huge difference in setting an athlete apart from their peers. *Athletic form* describes the proper technique and time-tested body mechanics that an athlete should use while trying to accomplish a specific task in sports.

For instance, there is a generally agreed upon form for throwing a football, performing a standing back tuck, shooting a lacrosse ball, and basically any other sports action. Form may differ slightly athlete to athlete, but the basics of that form are the same.

When teaching footwork and form, it can be difficult to know where to start, especially if you are not an expert in your child's sport of choice. Again, hiring a trainer is an option, but make sure that that trainer specializes in teaching the skills your child needs to work on, emphasizing the form and footwork of that skill.

Alternatively, I encourage you to find free and affordable resources online. Search for drills that can help your child improve their form and footwork as they develop those skills. So many elite athletes and trainers who do things the right way offer free training videos on sites like YouTube.

Consider filming your child while they practice and helping them to dissect the minor adjustments they might need to make to improve. Ask your child to invite those who do know the sport to give them feedback on their form and footwork. This will

take humility and coachability on their part, but it is essential
to improving.

Take Angel for example:

*Angel is a tenth grader with a passion for track and field and a ton of
raw talent. In particular, he has excelled at the long jump and competes
at the varsity level in the event. In his freshman year, he made it to the
county finals, finishing second overall. Now leading up to his sophomore
season, Angel has his mind set on medaling in the state championship. His
coach informs him that if he wants to compete at that level, he will have
to greatly improve his footwork and form in the long jump, particularly
when it comes to his run-up.*

*Angel's father—despite knowing little about the long jump—offers to
help him if Angel will look up training videos from some top athletes in
the event. Angel finds a video of an Olympic medalist doing a long-jump
tutorial and shows it to his dad. As the two compare Angel's form with
the video, they realize that he lacks consistency in his foot placement on
the run-up and also is not driving his free knee up enough on his takeoff.
Armed with this information, Angel starts to practice these elements of
footwork and form while his dad encourages and films him. Afterwards,
they look at the film together and celebrate where Angel has improved while
taking note of where he can still make some adjustments.*

This is a good example of how you can be a help to your
child even if you are not an expert in the sport yourself. Angel's
dad encourages his son to pursue growth and is by his side when

he needs him. Angel's father doesn't do the work for him, but encourages Angel and offers to help.

Sometimes our kids just need to know we are with them in it and have their back. This will be key as your daughter or son works on developing their skills as an athlete.

VISION

Once when I was talking with baseball hall-of-famer Ken Griffey Jr., he told me that the secret to him being such a prolific home-run hitter had to do with vision. Ken explained that upon the pitcher's release of the ball, he was able to identify the type of pitch based on seeing the rotation of the virgules, the red stitches along the seams of a baseball. Ken had seen every kind of pitch so often throughout his life that he had developed a type of *baseball vision*, where he could identify where the ball was heading the instant it left the pitcher's hand.

This kind of vision is not about having good eyesight, but about developing good intuition.

Athletic vision describes what happens when, during athletic competition, an athlete is able to see a given situation, understand what is going on, and identify the best course of action all within a split second. Another term it is known by is *sports IQ.*

Wayne Gretzky put it this way, "A good hockey player plays where the puck is. A great hockey player plays where the puck is going to be."

Those with great athletic vision can see things before they are going to happen. They have such an understanding of the game, themselves, their teammates, and their opponents that they can accurately predict outcomes and navigate the most difficult situations.

Vision is very difficult to teach. It involves memorizing every inch of the field of play, knowing the elaborate strategies and how to counter those strategies, developing impeccable and instantaneous discernment, thinking steps ahead of the rest while at the same time being grounded in the moment.

In short, athletes with great vision are playing chess while everyone else is playing checkers.

This kind of vision only can develop if an athlete is a dedicated student of the game. It means playing, watching, and studying the sport that they want to dedicate themselves to. This may sound a little intense, but when it is really what you love, the sport fascinates you and draws you in. It is still hard work, but it is hard work that is enjoyed.

Helping your kid develop vision starts with just watching the game and explaining to them what is going on. Help them understand why great athletes make certain decisions, listen to good commentators, and watch videos of great sports tacticians explaining the games beneath the game. Have them study the teachings of the great minds in their sports of choice and encourage them to study the sports theory behind that sport. Help them to fall in love with learning about the game so that they may approach it with an ever-growing level of understanding.

Teach them to become lifelong learners in sports (and in all things).

Furthermore, athletes with great vision are able to play by feel and instinct. During a game, they are not thinking about things like balance, footwork, and form because they have practiced those aspects so much that they do it without thinking. An athlete cannot get to that point unless they work on these essential skills ad nauseam.

If they put in the work, they can then start to learn and grow in their vision within the game itself. This is what makes great athletes turn into the best athletes.

A QUICK NOTE ON CREATIVITY

With all this stress on repetition and doing things the right way, our daughters and sons may feel as though we are squeezing all the fun out of sports and the creativity that comes with just going out there and playing.

Before we move on from this chapter, let me just say that I love creativity and the improvisational spirit with which so many young athletes approach sports. I in no way want to stifle that aspect of the athletic journey.

I would just point out that in jazz, only the most practiced musicians are able to improvise well.

The same is true for sports. You find more freedom to improvise in athletic competition when you bring all of the skills you have been working so hard to develop together in a unique way to meet the need of the moment. Creativity then becomes about being able to create the perfect combination of everything you have practiced in order to perfectly handle the uniqueness of a game-time situation. And when our physical skills are able to keep up with whatever our imagination can come up with, the game becomes immensely fun to play.

If your daughter or son wants to excel as an athlete, skill development is indispensable. As you consider how to help them accomplish their athletic dreams, this will be a practice to empha-size early and often.

CHAPTER 7

RAISING A GOOD TEAMMATE

One of the best teammates I ever had was a man by the name of Leonard "Len" Bias. Basketball fans may know him as the college basketball hall-of-famer who in 1986 was touted to be the next great professional basketball player.

I knew him as Lenny or LB.

Some NBA scouts at the time projected that Lenny would eventually be competing with the likes of Michael Jordan—a third-year player who had taken the league by storm—for supremacy as the NBA's best player.

Tragically, Len's life was cut short not long after he was drafted by the Boston Celtics as the second overall pick. The situation surrounding his death was sad and complex, and often steals the spotlight from the man himself. I, however, have chosen instead to focus on his life, the person he was, and how he treated me with kindness.

You see, when I first showed up at the University of Maryland, Lenny was going into his senior season, a superstar destined for greatness. As a junior, he led the ACC in scoring and was named the conference's player of the year—a huge feat considering we competed against the likes of the North Carolina Tar Heels and Duke Blue Devils.

Despite Len's success, he still took time to care about his teammates, even a freshman from Ohio who was yet to accomplish anything on the collegiate level. I was fresh from Wilmington when Lenny took me and my roommate, Dave Dickerson, under his wing.

On the court, his leadership was obvious and he was the embodiment of a great teammate. "Come on, G! Pick it up, baby!" he'd say, with equal parts encouragement and challenge. I knew he believed in me—which was powerful coming from perhaps the best player in the nation. In those calls, Len was attempting to awaken in me my best self on the court.

But it was the kind of teammate he continued to be off the court that really stood out. I can still hear his familiar "Y'all doing alright?" as he popped by our dorm room. Being from the nearby DC area, Lenny would take it on himself to watch out for us freshmen and make sure we had everything we needed. Dave Dickerson, Tony Massenburg, John Johnson, and I were all out-of-towners— from South Carolina, Virginia, Tennessee, and Ohio.

Len cared about the freshmen who had nothing and knew nothing. And as a result, we would do anything for Lenny. Not that getting our loyalty was his motive. You see, Len Bias seemed to understand something about being a teammate that a lot of athletes in this overly competitive sports culture do not realize.

Being a good teammate, first and foremost, is about being intentional.

This kind of teammate is hard to come by, and the development of this kind of teammate is often hindered by team cultures that are more focused on individual achievement than the success of the team. Especially as your daughter or son climbs to higher levels in their sport, there will be noticeably greater team competition for spots and positions. If a team is not intentional about making a selfless team-focused environment, healthy team culture can easily erode.

The healthiest teams have a culture similar to that of a healthy family. You will not always agree with your family, get along with your family, or even like your family. But family always has each other's backs as they each and all strive to do what is best for their family members.

If one member of the family is thinking and acting selfishly, the whole system is at risk of collapsing. This, as always, is a principle for life as well as sports.

As successful athletes, our daughters and sons have a responsibility to help create this sort of culture on the teams they are a part of. Now, it cannot fall solely on their shoulders, but they will carry a big weight because of their success.

In this chapter we will look at ways that we can teach our daughters and sons to be quality teammates and, in the process, quality friends.

IT'S ALL ABOUT RELATIONSHIPS

No matter the context, quality relationships are the cornerstone of a healthy team.

Despite this clear reality, I often see quality relationships ignored on teams—the sports variety or otherwise—in favor of transactional or production-focused relationships. These latter types of relationships tend to be one-sided and create an environment of looking out for one's self. As a result, production suffers, because no one is willing to do what is best for the other person and for the team.

And it is no wonder as to why. Quality relationships require something of us. Like all things of value, they take energy, effort, and work. But if our daughters and sons want to truly be good teammates, pursuing quality relationships with those on their teams is required.

The key to a quality relationship is seeing someone as a person first and foremost. Often we unthinkingly approach some we are connected to with an agenda or a lack of intentional care for who they are, while reserving our quality relationship energy for those we value most. This does not make us mean people necessarily, but it can cause us to act self-focused, always unconsciously asking, "What can this person do for me?" Rather, our question in pursuing quality relationships should be, "How can we both serve one another?"

In Lenny's interactions with Dave Dickerson and me, it was clear that he cared about us as human beings. He wanted to make sure we felt welcome, seen, and that our stomachs were full. Isn't this what we all want from each other? Someone to notice and care about the things we do?

Now I am not saying your child has to be best friends with everyone. We are all unique and are drawn to different people for different reasons. There are, however, ways to approach every one of your teammates with the intention of forming a quality relationship. It will, as in all things, take intentionality and practice for your child to make this approach to relationships a habit, but once it is ingrained in them, they will find that they are the kind of person that others are drawn to and trust.

These few practices, when pursued and incorporated into their relationships, will help our children grow into those types of people: the ones who see inherent value in each and every person and look to give to relationships as much as they receive.

COMMUNICATION

In our practice facility here with the Mavericks, there are various pillars around the practice courts that support the building. One day while walking through the facility, I noticed taped to one of the pillars was an eight-and-a-half-by-eleven-inch sheet of paper with a short message printed on it:

Communication can make or break any relationship.

This simple message had been hung by the championship head coach of the Dallas Mavericks at that time, Rick Carlisle, for players who passed by to read. Noticing that each pillar was adorned by its own sheet of paper, I moved around the room to see what each said. To my surprise, they all contained the same message: *Communication can make or break any relationship.* The same message, over and over again.

It was no accident that this phrase was taped to the pillars that kept the very building above our heads from crumbling. Coach Carlisle's message was clear. Communication was what will hold up this team—the Dallas Mavericks organization as a whole—and without it, we surely would crumble to the ground. If we want our kids to succeed in relationships of all kinds, including with their teammates, it behooves us to help them to communicate well, both on and off the playing field.

To understand good communication, we have to understand first what is involved. There are three main parts of communication: the message, the sender, and the receiver. One should consider (1) the **message** they want to communicate, (2) how they can best **send** that message, and (3) how the other person will best **receive** that message. In order for our children to communicate well, they have to keep all three aspects in mind.

Here is an example,

Tanner is a tenth-grade tennis player who loves to compete in doubles. Unfortunately, Tanner's former partner has moved out of state. Tanner's new partner, Elijah, is really talented, but the two are struggling to find chemistry and complement each other's playing style. Tanner is used to his communication style with his old partner, where certain looks and hand gestures could iron out any on-court struggles.

Tanner approaches Elijah about the issue in a friendly way after a match. Elijah reveals to his teammate that because Tanner is often quiet and reserved on the court, he believed Tanner to be constantly frustrated with Elijah's play. Elijah thinks it might help for them to connect, briefly strategize, and encourage each other in between points, believing this might help them to start to play better as a team. Tanner, being more reserved in nature, never thought of that sort of in-between-point communication and agrees that it is a good idea.

In this example, Tanner (the sender) is repeatedly sending messages that Elijah (the receiver) isn't getting. In fact, because of the way Tanner is communicating, Elijah is getting a completely different message (that Tanner is frustrated with him). In order for Tanner to get the message he wants to send across to Elijah, he has to touch base with his teammate and find a style of communication that will work for both of them.

Teaching our kids this, as always, starts at home, with our own communication with our child and other members of our family. We, as parents, must model good communication and gently yet clearly guide and correct our children's communication.

Also, encourage your child to communicate with teammates off the court. Have them shoot a quick text message or jump on video chat just to check in with teammates. Technology has made communication so easy these days, there is really no excuse. The lines of communication built outside of sports often translates back to the game.

Even if they are not the outspoken type, have them find a way that suits their unique personality in order to build strong lines of communication with each member of their team. Encourage them to use who they uniquely are for the good of the team. It is all the little ways you make an effort to communicate well that make a big difference in the long run and ultimately lead to quality relationships.

Then when conflict arises—and it will arise—your kid now has a strong line of communication to help work through it with that specific person, rather than being forced to rely on more unproductive strategies, such as exploding with anger or allowing an issue to fester.

ENCOURAGEMENT

In 2011, the Dallas Mavericks defeated the heavily-favored, LeBron James-led Miami Heat in the NBA Finals, four games to two. Despite being repeatedly underestimated—with NBA legend Dirk Nowitzki as their only All-Star—the Mavericks overcame the odds, becoming world champions for the first time in team history.

Though many may wonder how this unassuming team was able to triumph over a Miami team with three clear future hall-of-famers—LeBron, Dwyane Wade, and Chris Bosh—I was not so surprised. I was not working for the Mavs at that time, but did watch the team play all season long. No, they did not have a team full of All-Stars in their prime—though they certainly had plenty of underestimated talent. But they had something that talent could not supply: they were filled to the brim with incredible teammates.

In fact, *The Wall Street Journal* released an article[27] during these same NBA finals, outlining their analytics of team connection. "The Touchy-Feely Index," as they comedically called it, tracked on camera high fives, chest pats, butt slaps, and other forms of *athletic affection*. They found that, "The Mavericks, with 250 slaps,

---

27 Scott Cacciola, "Dallas's Secret Weapon: High Fives," *The Wall Street Journal*, June 9, 2011, https://www.wsj.com/articles/SB10001424052702304392704576373641168929846.

hugs, taps or bumps, are almost twice as touchy-feely as the Heat," and that "the Mavericks were 82% more likely to high five."[28]

Obviously, these analytics were simply an external sign to an internal reality. The Dallas Mavericks were a team united by quality relationships marked by persistent encouragement. This led to unparalleled team confidence and chemistry that was leveraged into an incredible championship season.

That Maverick team understood that one of the most important forms of communication on any team is mutual encouragement.

To encourage someone literally means to *put in* or *infuse courage* into that person. You can think about it as teammates loaning out their courage to those who, in some specific moment, may lack their own. We've all experienced this phenomenon. When everyone is committed to encouragement, the team environment changes. It becomes one filled with confidence and a willingness to give everything for the people who are fighting by your side. When a group is there to catch you when you fall, and lift you when you are down, you feel as though you can take on the world together.

This, again, is not about fancy speeches or always having the right words. It's the little encouragements that add up over time to shape the culture. It is the high fives and flying shoulder bumps. It is the quick acknowledgements as simple as pointing to a teammate or shouting "good pass!" It is the reassurance given when a teammate is down. Statements like *you'll get it next time, you got this,* and *don't worry, we got your back*!

---

28 Cacciola, "Dallas's Secret Weapon."

Like all communication, encouragement can be tailored to a specific receiver. Some teammates will prefer private acknowledgment, while public affirmation will mean the world to another. Teach your kids to ask themselves, *What does this person need to hear and how do they need to hear it?*

If you notice your child not acting with encouragement, kindly follow up with them after the game or practice. Suggest ways they can acknowledge and encourage their teammates on the court.

Extended off the court, this looks like being an encouraging friend. It is about being authentically available to those you are in relationship with. That means thinking of them, standing ready to be by their side, showing up when they need someone, and being present and authentic when with that person.

If a teammate of your child's is noticeably upset after the game, encourage your child to reach out and check in on them. If a teammate was injured during a game or practice that day, have them send a quick text of encouragement. If you know a teammate of your child is going through a personal trial, suggest your kid pick up a smoothie and take it to them at their house.

Another part of creating an encouraging culture is teaching your kids to look at the world and their team through a positive lens. Positive people believe in others in a way that a person led by negativity cannot. They see opportunities where others see obstacles, hope where others see hurdles. Not only do people love being around those who are positive, but positivity is also a useful tool for building others up as a form of encouragement.

This doesn't mean shrugging off important issues—we've already talked about the importance of working through conflict. Rather, positivity is the practice of emphasizing what you *can* do versus what you cannot.

The best way I have found to stay positive is to stay prepared. I am able to emphasize what we can accomplish as a team because I know we have put in the work required. The positive person models this type of preparation by making sure they themselves are ready, and by inviting others to follow them into that readiness. And, as we will explore in the next section, for the successful athlete, this kind of leadership is not optional.

SELFLESS LEADERSHIP

Perhaps the most important practice of a good teammate is their willingness to give of themselves selflessly for those they are competing alongside.

I think part of the reason youth sports participation has dropped over the last decade is due to the *me mentality* that has taken hold in our culture. So many young athletes have become swept up in their own success, their own fulfillment, and their own self-centered entitlement that they rarely have much energy to offer their teammates.

This is highly problematic. Not only is it a losing strategy in sports, but it is a losing strategy in life. A self-centered mentality corrodes everything it touches, whether one's family, friendships, marriage, or career.

It is the classic crabs-in-a-bucket analogy. If multiple crabs are in a small bucket together, and one crab tries to escape, the other crabs will pull the escaping crab back into the bucket in hopes that they can climb over their fellow crab's back and get out themselves. Since all the crabs are only worried about their own escape, none of them can escape.

Similarly, selfish teammates can sabotage each other, keeping their teammates from reaching their true potential while at the same time hindering their own personal elevation. The only way to *short-circuit* this sort of behavior on a team is for one or more leaders on the team to lower themselves in order to lift up their teammates.

As a successful athlete, your child will be a leader to some extent simply because they will have others who look to them and follow them, if only for their talent. There are always people watching and imitating, whether you like it or not. The difference between being a good leader and a leader who tears others and themself down is selflessness. Thus, selfless leadership is vital for successful athletes.

Former United States Secretary of State, Colin Powell, once said that "good leaders are people who are trusted by followers."[29] He went on to say that the only real way to build that trust is through selfless service.

Think about it. Who are the people you trust the most? Those that you would do anything for? Are they not the people who have been there, who have given up their own good for your betterment?

---

29 Colin Powell, "The Essence of Leadership," posted by jjbpaca on YouTube, 2011, video, https://www.youtube.com/watch?v=ocSwlm30UBI.

They are parents, grandparents, spouses, siblings, and best friends. Sacrifice and service breed trust in a quality relationship.

And sacrificial leaders help their team see the importance of lowering themselves for the sake of elevating their teammates. So much of this comes back to humility—seeing yourself and others rightly. Selflessness reminds us that we should see ourselves and others as the valuable human beings we are.

Now this doesn't mean our daughters and sons have to lose their edge. But selfishness is also antithetical to the sort of fierce competition we are talking about. If anyone thinks they are deserving of or entitled to something just because they walk on the field, they neglect the basic principle that everything in athletic competition must be earned.

That is why selfishness should not be tolerated in sports or at home. Help your child to understand that the world is not all about them. Let us model selflessness for our children and let it be an expectation we have of them. Help them to understand that they are accountable to their teammates and coaches when it comes to their actions, attitude, the work they put in, and the way they show up at a game or practice. They are accountable, because their decisions have an impact on others, especially those on their team.

Quick side note for any coaches reading this: I don't care how good a player is; if they are only about themselves, they are a detriment to your whole team. Either set them straight or allow them to move on.

Selfless athletes grow into selfless employees, bosses, spouses, and parents, and selflessness is the only antidote to the disease of a team full of self-centered individuals. Your daughter or son cannot do it alone, but leaders do what is necessary when no one else will. Our children cannot wait for someone else to step up—or in this case, kneel down. Their teams and our futures depend on it.

CHAPTER 8

LIVING THE BALANCED LIFE

Hall of Fame basketball legend Alonzo Mourning once said to me, "If your body is your business, you better take care of it." This statement carried tremendous weight coming from 'Zo. You see, in 2000, he learned that he had a rare and potentially deadly kidney disorder. The same disorder had ended many athletes' careers in the past and it now threatened to do the same for the seven-time NBA All-Star.

However, after a double kidney transplant in 2003, 'Zo overcame the odds and returned to the court in 2004. Not only did he return, but 'Zo continued to play at a high level and was even a part of the 2006 Miami championship team.

Today Alonzo knows the importance of a healthy and balanced life and has dedicated a big part of his life to educating others about healthy living and raising awareness around kidney disease. He is very conscious about his nutrition and lifestyle, never taking his health for granted.

Sadly, the importance of taking care of your body is a lesson many athletes do not learn until much later in life. What is even more rare is a young athlete who has a sense of healthy living beyond the physical dimension.

In order to live a truly balanced life, one must consider health in all its arenas: physical health, mental-emotional health, social health, financial health, and even spiritual health.

In this chapter, we will look at the importance of health in all these areas and how our daughters and sons can learn to embrace this balanced lifestyle at an early age. In this, we are of course setting them up for success in sports, but, as always, this is more about setting them up for *life*.

As you read this chapter, you may yourself be challenged by its content. This chapter is in no way meant to shame your lifestyle or that of your children. It is simply about emphasizing how important health is for you and your family.

Of course, none of us can live a perfectly healthy life. Know that there is room for grace and growth all along this journey. I know these aspects of healthy living continue to challenge me to be better for myself and for my daughters. But if we are not even working towards these goals, what ground can be made in the area of health? And the fact remains that our health, or lack of health, has an impact on our kids for better and worse.

My hope in this chapter, though, is to present some thoughts that can help you and your whole family strive to live a well-balanced life of health and wholeness. Without this goal set before us and our kids, true well-roundedness in sports and life will feel forever just out of reach.

PHYSICAL HEALTH

When my daughters were growing up, we made physical health a huge priority. We, as a family, tried to emphasize regular exercise, proper rest, and healthy eating. Though none of us are perfect at this, we have all learned to embrace this lifestyle of caring for our bodies and it continues to be a priority for each of us today.

I've already written extensively about the importance of both rest and exercise in previous chapters, so I want to take this opportunity to talk about the importance of nutrition.

A position statement released by the American College of Sports Medicine states that "the performance of, and recovery from, sporting activities are enhanced by well-chosen nutrition strategies."[30] I'd venture to say that an athlete's performance and recovery is *greatly* enhanced by well-chosen nutrition strategies, especially when considering the long-term effects of a consistently healthy or unhealthy diet.

Athletes of every age need to understand that their body in some ways runs like a car—the fuel you put into it will directly impact the way that engine runs. If you are constantly feeding your engine with junky fuel—say nachos and soda from the gym snack bar—it will, in turn, feel sluggish and low-energy. But when you consistently fill your tank with high-octane fuel—complex carbohydrates, healthy fats, and proteins—you will be able to perform to your full potential.

---

30 American Dietetic Association, Dietitians of Canada, American College of Sports Medicine, et al; American College of Sports Medicine position stand, "Nutrition and athletic performance," *Medicine and Science in Sports and Exercise* 40, no. 3 (March, 2009): 709-731. https://doi.org/10.1249/mss.0b013e31890eb86.

In order for young kids to learn to value the nutrition that comes with a healthy diet, we as parents must serve as models and encouragers. There are many worthwhile disciplines that you can incorporate in your home that will set your children up for success. These include:

- purging your fridge and cupboards of unhealthy snacks with high sucrose (empty sugar), such as candies, baked sweets, ice cream, sodas, and sports drinks,

- staying well stocked with healthier snacks, such as fruits and vegetables,

- packing snacks and lunches when going to athletic events and avoiding eating out when possible,

- committing to no sugar added and no fast food during the season,

- and doing a little online research and coming up with a realistic family nutrition plan that you all can commit to together.

Also, remind your kids that nutrition is about health and about *feeling* your best. Consider Rachel's story:

Rachel is a talented junior wrestler who is thriving in tournaments across the region. She has already won more than one coed tournament this season and is poised to compete in the female state tournament at the 111-pound weight class. In an attempt to stay in her current weight class, Rachel is extremely strict about what she eats. Her parents at first see this as a strength, but a routine physical reveals that Rachel is substantially underweight given her increase in height. The doctor would not normally worry, but when hearing of Rachel's meager diet, how she often skips lunch, and that she has even passed out in practice on one occasion, the doctor calls on Rachel and her parents to make some changes. Rachel is reluctant at first, but her parents talk to her about how important her nutrition is and encourage her to not be afraid of wrestlers in higher weight classes. Rachel agrees that a new, more balanced nutrition regimen is what is best, and starts to make the changes she needs to be her best, healthiest self.

In this example, Rachel has confused limiting her food intake with healthy nutrition. Just as Rachel's parents did, we must help our children find a balanced nutrition plan—not consisting of over- *or* under-eating. Some things to steer them away from are scale-watching, weight obsession, fad diets, comparison to others, and overemphasis on body shape.

These are serious issues that our young people face, and shame-based strategies will do them far more harm than good. Keep your conversations around nutrition nonspecific—not directly focusing on them—and help them see that this is something you are doing as an entire family to lead healthier lives.

MENTAL-EMOTIONAL HEALTH

In recent years, many top professional athletes have taken it upon themselves to speak up about what some call a *mental health crisis* in our society. The likes of Aly Raisman, Andrew Luck, DeMar DeRozan, Abby Wambach, and Kevin Love (to name a few) have spoken of their own mental health struggles in an attempt to destigmatize and encourage others to seek help.

According to a study about the mental disorders in American adolescents, almost a third of teens meet the criteria for anxiety disorder, nearly 20% for behavioral disorders, and there are substantial percentages experiencing mood or substance-use disorders.[31] Student athletes also identify significant stressors associated with athletic performance, parental satisfaction, balancing academics, and finding their identity in sports.[32]

Mental-emotional unhealth is a significant problem that should be taken seriously in an athlete's journey. For serious mental health issues, it is important that we seek the guidance of mental health professionals, but there are ways we can also help contribute positively to our child's mental health.

Again, proper rest, nutrition, and exercise all can contribute positively to a person's overall mental-emotional state, but there are also other practices that can be extremely helpful in setting our daughters and sons up for health in this area.

First is healthy conversation and a connection with you as a parent. I have had conversations with young athletes who feel they are at the end of their energy and the anxiety of what they are going through feels too difficult to cope with. I cannot help

31 Kathleen Ries Merikangas, Jian-Ping He, Marcy Burstein, Sonja A. Swanson, Shelli Avenevoli, Lihong Cui, Corina Benjet, Katholiki Georgiades, Joel Swendsen, "Lifetime prevalence of mental disorders in US adolescents: results from the National Comorbidity Survey Replication–Adolescent Supplement (NCS-A)," *Journal of the American Academy of Child and Adolescent Psychiatry* (July 31, 2010, epub): https://pubmed.ncbi.nlm.nih.gov/20855043/.

32 Timothy L. Neal et al., "Interassociation Recommendations for Developing a Plan to Recognize and Refer Student-Athletes With Psychological Concerns at the Secondary School Level: A Consensus Statement," *Journal of Athletic Training* 50, no. 3 (2015): 232, https://www.nata.org/sites/default/files/developing_a_plan_to_recognize_and_refer_student_athletes_with_psychological_concerns_at_the_college_level.pdf.

we some was about putting some away even if my girls didn't
what they were saving for. This money could be used for
purchase—rather than us as parents simply buying it for
—or stored away just because. Again, the amount is less
rtant than the practice.

nd, finally, they got to *spend some*. They could use this spend-
oney to do something fun with friends or family. Fun has
s been a big value in our family and I wanted my daughters
ow that it is okay to spend money on healthy fun regularly.
the movies, the roller rink, an amusement park. Get out
ave a good time with friends. That doesn't mean breaking
nk for something foolish, but it just means that setting aside
money to have fun is an important practice.

s our daughters and sons get older, we can start to introduce
financial responsibility. This means more money, of course,
so more expenses. Have them budget some of this additional
y to pay for their gas and their cell phone bill. Don't just
atically pay these costs, but let them know that it is *their*
sibility to set aside enough money to pay for gas and their
one. This teaches them the importance of paying their bills.
t them know that there is always food in the cupboard that
ill provide for them, but if they want to buy something to
school or at a nearby restaurant, that should come out of
monthly stipend. Then when you take them out on your
it is a treat and not a given.

d if they spend all of their stipend, try not to bail them out.
do not have money for gas, have them schedule a ride with

but have compassion for them as often young people are working
through very real emotions both in sports and outside of it.

The way we show up as parents in these moments is
critical. Anxiety, depression, and other mental disorders
can often serve as a check engine light pointing to bigger
issues in our lives. Even when our emotions do not match
the reality of our situations, the experience of these feelings is
very real. We must allow our children a safe space to express what
they are feeling.

We also need to reflect thoughtfully about how much pressure
we are putting on our daughter or son and their athletic journey.
If our own identity is wrapped around our child being an athlete
in some way, they can feel as though they are carrying an immense
weight in their family. If them desiring to put down sports for a
time feels devastating to us as parents, there is a problem.

Other simple practices can include limiting screen time (especially with our young children), encouraging healthy friendships,
and helping them build an identity outside of sports. These aspects
are a subcategory of mental-emotional health that some think of
as *social health*.

Promoting our kids' social health can look like encouraging
our kids towards other social activities beyond athletics. The
professionalization of youth sports is a real issue and it is important
to help our kids fight against it. This means allowing them space
for school involvement such as going to dances, attending sporting
events they are not involved in, and being with their peers in other
ways. It might mean involvement in the community or in their

local religious youth group. These social aspects of childhood are vastly undervalued.

Another helpful practice when it comes to mental health is taking the time to serve others with your children. Giving back with our time and energy can have a remarkable impact on our own mental-emotional outlook, as well as benefitting those we serve. Check out what opportunities are available through the local food bank, soup kitchen, or religious organization. This is something to do as a family and an awesome opportunity to model compassion, understanding, and kindness for our children, even at a young age.

Again, if you or your child are having serious difficulty in the area of mental-emotional health, I cannot encourage you enough to seek the guidance of a mental health professional. I'll end this section with a powerful quote from sixteen-time Olympic medalist (and thirteen-time *gold* medalist) Michael Phelps, speaking on his severe depression:

For the longest time, I thought asking for help was a sign of weakness because that's kind of what society teaches us. That's especially true from an athlete's perspective. If we ask for help, then we're not this big macho athlete that people can look up to. Well, you know what? If someone wants to call me weak for asking for help, that's their problem. Because I'm saving my own life.

FINANCIAL HEALTH

Financial health, or financial literacy, is also ant aspect of the balanced life. Many of our included, are growing up with little to no prepare them for adulthood—not to mentic cial opportunities and dangers that will fac to play professionally.

As parents we want to take the time to and sons in the way of financial wisdom as we are helping them to build discipline

One of my favorite sayings in the bibl trusted with very little can also be trusted wi is dishonest with very little will also be dish

With our daughters, we started them off to learn basic financial skills with a little mo as helping them open a bank account, gi stipend or allowance, and helping them to

Early in their lives, the budget consisted gories: give some, save some, spend some.

Give some meant that generosity was son be on the forefront of our mind as a famil school, we taught our girls to give back—in we attended. For your children, you may w out a worthy charity that they can regularl is not as important as the practice.

Those who give as children will give as

33 Luke 16:10, NIV.

you on *your* time or have them find a ride with a friend. They can do a couple chores around the house to pay off their phone bill. No money for lunch? Pack something from the fridge.

Help them to see that with real responsibility comes real consequences.

Later in life, you can give them some money for stock options, teach them how to navigate the market, talk to them about the dangers of consumer debt, and discuss other complex issues. This is about preparing them for life after (and in some cases during) sports.

If you yourself need to take a financial literacy class, I encourage you to do so. There are affordable online options and it is well worth the investment. Also, there are tons of books on the subject. That is how I learned about the importance of saving, stock options, IRAs, 401(k)s, and emergency funds.

SPIRITUAL HEALTH

The final area of a balanced life that I want to highlight for you is spiritual health. No matter your spiritual beliefs, I have found paying attention to our spirituality can add another layer of health to our lives in deeply impactful ways. A healthy spiritual life can be a source of unspeakable joy, strength, hope, and comfort.

For me personally, I have found it so important to have a higher power to lean on during the good times and during the bad times. My faith has made my highest highs even better and has guided me through my lowest lows.

Perhaps there was no lower point in my life than when I lost both my father and brother in a boating accident. I was only twenty-two at the time, had just graduated college, and was ready to dive into my new season of life. The obviously devastating situation would have been nearly impossible to get through if it wasn't for the support of my family and my God.

From this experience, I know that when my own strength fails, God will never leave me and his strength is enough.

I pray that your children never have to face such pain, but I do know that adversity in life is unavoidable. It will not always be as severe as an unexpected death, but there will, without doubt, be peaks and valleys in our lives, athletic journeys included. Whether it is a difficult relationship with a coach or teammate, a chronic or devastating injury, or just a slump, there is so much that can go wrong all along the way.

A healthy spiritual life can give us strength to pick ourselves up again when we feel like we cannot and something beyond ourselves to cling to when we are at the end of our rope. It gives us the ability to approach things out of our control with peace and surrender. Spiritual health teaches us that some of the most difficult situations might hold opportunities for tremendous growth in our lives if we approach them with open eyes and open hands.

Obviously, this is something for you and your family to unpack together, but I do encourage exploration in this area. Walk with your kids in this and talk with them about spiritual things. I hope your family will find in it the same blessing that my family and I have.

THE BALANCED LIFE

The truly balanced life can only come when *all* these areas are a priority. Though we separate and individualize all these areas of health, we are more like an ecosystem, interconnected and intertwined. Each of these areas of health impact the others, and anemic areas will influence health across the board. What we are after is a holistic health for ourselves and our daughters and sons.

Sports can be a conduit for this kind of health, and grow us far beyond physical vitality. As US Soccer star and two-time Olympic gold medalist Julie Foudy says, "Sports not only build better athletes, but also better people."

CHAPTER 9

PREPARING FOR THE NEXT LEVEL

Though there is a lot for athletes to be excited about when taking the leap to collegiate level athletics, the transition can feel quite overwhelming for those who are unprepared. The game is faster, the stakes higher, and the competition more fierce—not to mention that the athlete will face all this while trying to balance a university-level academic load. Oh, and most college athletes will also be living away from home for the first time.

Sports anchor at The Athletic and former Duke tennis player, Prim Siripipat, sums up these dueling tensions of college sports well,

> My college experience was rewarding, but it was one of the most difficult periods of my life. I struggled to juggle the responsibilities of being a student athlete. The perfectionist in me was trying to keep up with my peers in the classroom and my teammates of our top-10 team.[34]

There is so much that can leave our daughters and sons feeling in over their heads. That is why so much of this book is about setting your child up for success *before* they go off to university.

34 Prim Siripipat, "Moving on from Sports: A College Athlete's Greatest Challenge," ESPN, ESPN Internet Ventures, April 11, 2016, https://www.espn.com/espnw/voices/story/_/id/15182997/moving-sports-college-athlete-greatest-challenge.

We spend hours teaching our children to train, study, and approach life with integrity and perseverance, we oversee the slow and deliberate transition to them managing their own schedule, responsibilities, and relationships, and we teach them to be intentional about their nutrition, rest, and discipline. All of this has been about preparing them to make healthy choices for themselves *when they no longer have us right by their side.*

If we have truly kept our primary objective in mind—raising a successful athlete who is also a healthy, successful, and socially responsible individual—then we can step into this transition to the next level with confidence that our daughters and sons are ready to face the rigors and challenges that being a collegiate student athlete will present.

In this chapter, we will be looking at some healthy and appropriate approaches we can take with our children when it comes to the recruitment process and the transition to college athletics.

EARLY RECRUITMENT

Collegiate athletic programs start building relationships with top-level athletes as early as seventh or eighth grade—though high school is a much more common time for this early courtship to take place. Letters may come in the mail, coaches may reach out, and maybe even a scout will show up to their game.

This type of attention is flattering and can even be an indicator of a young athlete's potential. Beyond that, however, it really does not mean much. At the end of the day, none of these things equate to a scholarship offer.

I sometimes see athletes and parents alike getting caught up in the excitement of receiving college interest letters. Some fall into the trap of bragging, comparing, and even competing with one another over how many letters they have received and from which universities.

At the end of the day, this behavior is frivolous and ultimately counterproductive for our kids and their goals. On the one hand, this can jeopardize the humility that you are working so hard to instill in them, and, on the other, it can place a tremendous amount of unnecessary pressure on them as they try to live up to these expectations.

Therefore, it is important that we help temper our daughter's or son's expectations when it comes to this early recruitment process, especially when they are young. Be honest with them about what these letters mean—a university wants to open a line of communication *just in case* you continue to develop into an athlete they believe would be a good fit for their program.

In some ways college athletic programs are hedging their bets. On the wide end of the funnel, these schools send out letters to many promising young athletes—many more than they actually have room for in their programs. Out of that larger pool, they track from a distance who is developing well, and, seeing this, they start to narrow that pool. In some ways the university is playing a numbers game, and it is important that we are honest with our kids about that.

Help them also to understand that so much can change over even a few years. They may get hurt, lose interest, stop growing, the head coach of an interested university may change, and so on. With so much still up in the air at this early recruitment stage, it is best to not allow this early attention to sidetrack your child from their greater goals.

I find it is best for athletes to use this sort of attention as a means of motivation to work even harder. Help them reframe things like letters with positive self-talk such as: *you can do this if you keep putting in the work* or *you are on the right path, now let's push to the finish line!*

VIEWING PERIOD

Following this wide-end-of-the-funnel early recruitment is a viewing period for interested programs to scout high school athletes. This may start with a request for some full game footage and some assistant coaches to come out to see an athlete play. As interest grows, coaches are evaluating athletes to see whether they may be a good fit for their university's program.

When I was an assistant with the women's basketball program at the University of Washington, we would often find some of our best recruits while watching another athlete. Once while scouting a highly recruited player in the Bay Area, I was introduced to a different athlete who played with such passion that she couldn't be ignored. Despite this, I was shocked to find that this talented young player was not being heavily recruited by the larger programs on the west coast. She could flat-out play. Handles, hustle, heart. We eventually offered her a scholarship to play with the Huskies and she accepted.

That unknown recruit grew into all-time Huskie great Jazmine Davis. Jazmine finished her career at UW as the program's all-time points leader and even played professionally for a time.

I tell this story to demonstrate how vital it is that athletes and parents alike represent themselves well at all times. You just never know who is in the gym at a given time. Unrecognized scouts, alumni, or friends of a given program may be in attendance, not to mention that coaches often like to keep a low profile when they attend games. Furthermore, it is not uncommon for scouts who are drawn to a game or tournament by a specific prospect to keep an eye out for other athletes that may fit well with their program—as I did with Jazmine.

Coaches are not only evaluating skills and talent, but also the more intangible attributes of an athlete. What kind of teammate and leader are they? Do they play hard on every possession, snap, or play? Are they coachable? How do they respond when they are having a bad game? Do they keep their head up, impact the game in other ways, and support their teammates? These characteristics speak volumes to a college coach.

Also, remind your daughter or son that recruiters will seek to learn about how they present themselves in contexts other than the court or field. Longtime North Carolina baseball coach, Mike Fox, points out how an athlete's classroom performance is weighed,

The very first thing we do after we see a young man play, is request his transcripts. That happens immediately and can be the first separator in determining whether we move forward with a young man. I think there's a direct correlation between how a young man performs in the classroom and the kind of commitment or self-discipline he has. We need young men that are prepared for college work, and most of the time, the transcripts tell the other side of the story.[35]

NCAA Division II Championship football coach, Colby Carthel, puts it this way,

Here's the deal: we are going to do our digging. If we're serious enough to recruit you, you better believe we are going to find out exactly who you are. We're going to talk to your coaches. We're going to talk to your teachers and your classmates.[36]

And if we think these coaches are not watching us parents as well, we are fooling ourselves. Coaches will be asking, *How are this athlete's parents interacting with their child, other parents, other players, coaches, and referees?* (Yes, how you speak to referees, umpires, and officials matters!) *Is this the type of parent I want to deal with for the next four years? What are the values of this family and will they fit with our program?*

That means we as parents have to be conscious of our own behavior and how we treat others. And if our true goal is our

---

35 Ross Hawley, "Recruiting Column: Quotes That Will Shape Your Recruiting Experience," USA TODAY High School Sports, March 23, 2018, https://usatodayhss.com/2018/recruiting-column-quotes-that-will-shape-your-recruiting-experience.

36 Hawley, "Recruiting Column," USA TODAY High School Sports.

children's growth as whole people anyway, it behooves us to be the people of respect, kindness, and self-control we hope our daughters and sons will be. When we lose sight of this goal, we not only send our children the wrong message, but also may be working against their dreams!

Furthermore, your response to your child after a college coach attends a game is very important. If you or your child notice a coach scouting a game, talk about it casually afterward. A high-profile coach on the sidelines can be nerve-racking for an athlete the first couple times. Give your daughter or son some grace if they didn't play well. The last thing they need is additional pressure.

If one or more schools believe your daughter or son could be a good fit for their program, you and your kid should have the chance to build some personal relationships with the coaching staff. If the head coach of a university has not personally reached out to you as a parent, that is a red flag. It is important to get to know the person who will be directly in charge of your child's well-being before your child commits to that particular program.

If this process goes well, your child may end up with some scholarship offers—though this is far from guaranteed. Though there are some cases of early offers, most scholarship offers come in an athlete's senior year. Offers or not, it is important that you help your daughter or son to make an informed decision when choosing where they want to attend college.

CHOOSING THE RIGHT SCHOOL

A lot of factors go into the decision of what university to attend. My daughter Jaime was fortunate enough to have various options when it came to playing at the collegiate level. To help her sort through her choices, I encouraged her to do a college vision board. A *college vision board* is a visual representation of a future student's priorities when choosing a university to attend.

In short, I asked her, *What would Jaime Nared University look like?*

I recommend you have your daughters or sons do this exercise, found at the end of this chapter, when they are considering their own college decisions. This works for athletes and non-athletes alike, so if you have a child who does not play sports, it can be worthwhile for them as well.

First, I had Jaime consider the various aspects of the college experience that mattered to her. Here are the kinds of questions I asked her: What major(s) interest you? What are the academic demands? What are your top priorities when it comes to the athletic program? What matters as far as the student life is concerned? Where in the country do you want to go to school? Do you want to be in a city or somewhere less busy?

Next, I had her rank all these aspects in order of importance to her. Your child can then use their vision board to highlight these aspects to make a visual representation of their imaginary dream school. This is a chance for them to dream big and have fun with it. They can use as much or as little creativity as they want; the important thing is they think about what really matters for them.

Once they have their dream school thought-out, they can look at their options and see how each school measures up to the dream. Have them do their own research, but make sure they are asking the right questions.

- **Academically:** *Does this school have the major that interests you? Where does that program rank in the nation? How does the school rank academically overall? What is the teaching style, average classroom size, and educational philosophy?*

- **Athletically:** *What is the coaching staff like? Did you research the head coach? What are their values and coaching style? How do teammates interact with each other? What year are the other players at your position? If they are underclassmen, do you want to compete with them your whole collegiate career? What conference do you want to play in?*

- **Student Life:** *Are they a big school with lots going on or a small school where it is easy to meet people? Do they have vibrant athletic programs? Do they have Greek life? What other opportunities do they have to meet people and have fun? How diverse is the campus? Does the school value diversity? How safe is the campus? What are the campus crime statistics? Do they have a highly ranked campus safety team?*

- **Location:** *How far is it from home? What is the weather like? What is the local population like? Is there stuff to do in the area? How safe is the area? What are the city crime statistics? Did you research local law enforcement?*

Prepared with this research, talk through each school with your daughter or son and see which few line up best with their dream school. This helps to teach them the value of making well thought-out decisions. At this point, I recommend narrowing it down to five at most.

The next step is for you and your child to visit each school. Reach out to the various coaches and see when would be the best time for a visit. Use these visits to continue to build relationships with these coaches.

Though you will be with your daughter or son, equip your daughter or son with the right questions to ask. Have them ask current players about the head coach and staff. *Do they lose their temper often? Are they a yeller? Do they pick on a certain player? Do you like playing for this coach/staff? What are their expectations? Can you walk me through a normal practice schedule? How do you like the school?*

Have them ask the head coach and staff about their family, their interests outside of coaching, if they are a person of faith, how they like working at the university, and how they got into coaching. The goal here is to get a sense for the kind of person this coach is and what they are really like.

Also have them pay attention to the nonverbal clues that present themselves on these visits. How do the coaches and players treat and interact with each other? Do current players take recruits to inappropriate events or parties? Do they pressure recruits to drink or engage in other behavior they are not comfortable with? Does the athletic program use morally questionable recruitment tactics? These can all be indicators of an unhealthy school environment for your daughter or son.

Also make sure you set up a meeting for you, your child, and an academic advisor while on the visit. Tour the rest of the campus and the facilities relevant to the major they are interested in. See if they can talk with a professor and some students that are a part of that department and get a feel for what that program is like.

At the end of the day, these visits are all a part of the learning and discernment process.

After these visits, your child should be armed with a good sense of their options and should be ready to make a good decision when the time comes. Though we as parents will have opinions about where our children go to school—and certainly it is good for us to voice those opinions in a non-pressuring way—ultimately the decision is our child's to make. Once your child has all the information they need and has narrowed down their list, the final decision usually comes down to their relationships with the head coach and staff.

THE NEXT LEVEL

Once a decision has been made, and our daughter or son starts their collegiate athletic career, the time comes for us as parents to let go. Most universities—especially in the context of a healthy athletic program—will provide students with a safe, semi-controlled environment in which to learn to truly take up the responsibilities of the real world.

Despite this, letting go still takes a lot of trust. Trust in God and in the way you have prepared your child for exactly this moment, to fully take the reins of their athletic journey and ultimately their life.

Our role then in their athletic journey becomes solely that of the encourager and supporter. Our attention can instead focus on making sure our daughter or son is safe, fed, prioritizing their education, and building new and lasting friendships.

This means they have to have their own conversations with teammates, coaches, and professors. Consider Isabella's story:

Isabella is a competitive cheerleader in her first semester at college. She is far from home, a bit overwhelmed with her school load, and feeling homesick. On top of this stress, Isabella is struggling to learn the many routines of her new squad. Despite really connecting with her head coach, Isabella is not used to his style of coaching. Frustrated, she reaches out to her parents for advice. They help her to calm down, encouraging Isabella to give herself grace. They remind her that new routines take time to master and that, if she works hard and has a positive attitude, they have no doubt she will learn them.

They also suggest Isabella have a conversation with her head coach about ways she might be able to pick up the new routines and improve. When she speaks with her head coach, he informs her that some of the other freshmen are having similar issues and they might benefit from working on the routines together after practice with one of the assistant coaches. Isabella agrees and starts the new after-practice regimen with the other freshmen and the assistant coach.

In this story, Isabella's parents both encourage and empower their daughter to step into her own journey and trust her own communication, relationship, and conflict-resolution skills. It may be tempting for her parents to step in, especially since their daughter has been stressed in other areas. But Isabella is able to resolve the conflict she is facing without her parents interceding on her behalf and thus will be stronger for it.

This is an example of appropriate parental support at college-level athletics. There is no reason for a parent to call the university or coaching staff on an athlete's behalf unless there is a safety concern.

If your daughter or son feel they are not getting the playing time they deserve, help them come up with a game plan on how to talk to the coach and figure out what they can do to improve. When they have a conflict with a teammate, talk with them about how to broach the subject in a nonconfrontational way. If they are struggling with their game, remind them of all the hard work that got them here and encourage them to keep being that kind of person. If they work hard, play their role, and are ready when their number is called, good things will come.

As parents, it can be tempting to want to rescue our kids or explain to a coach what would work best with our daughter or son. This is inappropriate. It is important that we parents leave the coaching to those who get paid to do the job. There is a reason they are coaching at this level. When challenges arise, as they undoubtedly will, the best thing we can do for our child is help them to figure out a solution for themselves.

So go to their game and just have fun cheering your kid on! Be there whether they are playing or not. The times they are not is when they will need your support the most. In this, we encourage them to fight their own battles, while assuring them that we will never leave their corner.

COLLEGE VISION BOARD EXERCISE

A college vision board is a visual representation of a future student's priorities when choosing a university to attend. This is a great exercise for all your kids, whether they are an athlete or not.

1. Take your kid down to the local arts and crafts store and pick up a poster board or science display board, along with some glue sticks and markers (if you don't have some at home already). At the top of the board, have them write their first and last names, followed by the word "University" (e.g. Jaime Nared University).

2. Have your kids consider the various aspects of the college experience that matter to them. Have them think about what their dream university would entail:

    a. What major(s) interest you? Where does that school's program rank amongst other schools?

    b. What is most important to you academically?

    c. What are your top priorities when it comes to the athletic program (or other program of interest)? E.g., a football program.

    d. What matters as far as the student life is concerned? Does the university have a diverse group of students? Do they have a football program or a bent towards the arts?

    e. Where in the country do you want to go to school? Do you want to be in a city or somewhere less busy?

    f. Who are your favorite head coaches? How do they operate?

    g. What kind of alumni network do you want to have access to? (This is for helping to find a job after graduation.)

3. Next, have your child rank all these aspects in order of importance to them. Then have them write each aspect on the board, leaving a

space below each aspect for images. They can put their most important aspect at the top or in the center, with less important aspects further down or around the edges.

4. *Finally, have them make a visual representation of their imaginary dream school by cutting out words and images that represent each aspect they wrote down from old magazines or newspapers and pasting them to the board. This is a chance for them to dream big and have fun with it. They can use as much or as little creativity as they want; the important thing is that they think about what really matters to them.*

5. *Once they have their dream school thought-out, they can look at their options and see how each school measures up to the dream. Have them do their own research, but make sure they are asking the right questions.*

CHAPTER 10

LIFE AFTER SPORTS

I was excited to be sitting directly across from the football hall-of-famer. I was a huge fan of this longtime NFL quarterback and we happened to be at the same small dinner event. We talked for some time about sports and life, and eventually our conversation settled on his experience since his retirement years earlier.

"What was the first year like out of football?" I asked curiously, not thinking much of the question.

The NFL legend, with emotion in his voice, replied, "I was in isolation for a whole year." I was shocked and saddened by this response. He elaborated, "I just didn't know what to do with myself. Couldn't even get out of bed. I missed football. Not the workouts, but being in the locker room with my friends. And Sundays. I miss the fans cheering me on and the joy that brought me."

I was floored by this revelation—that someone who had achieved such greatness had struggled so deeply. The man had been playing professionally for over two decades, and even before that his life had been all about football. Now, all of a sudden, he did not know who he was supposed to be.

This legendary player is not alone; this is an experience felt by many athletes, of all levels. No matter how good the athlete or how high they climb the ladder, one day their playing career will end.

Former Pro Bowl cornerback and executive vice president of football operations for the NFL Troy Vincent alluded to this struggle, saying, "You're talking about an identity crisis. Every athlete has to face the same question when they're done: 'Who am I?'"[37]

Longtime NFL running back Tiki Barber talked about it this way: "I realized how fast the opportunities disappear. You've been replaced on the field and you've been replaced in people's minds. That's when you start getting depressed."[38]

I still remember the internal conversation I had with myself when it became clear that my lifelong dream of playing in the NBA would never be realized. It was in the first half of my senior year at the University of Maryland that the reality that I would not be going pro sunk in. The upcoming season would be my last.

Like all loss, the loss of a dream comes in phases. Initially, I felt something equating to low-level shock. I kept repeating the phrase, *you are done*, to myself, trying to allow this truth to sink in. As it did, a feeling of emptiness accompanied it.

Being a basketball player was so much of who I was. Up until this point, sports had been at the center of my life—playing basketball or preparing for the next time I would play. Games, practice, training, being with teammates—this is how I spent the vast majority of my time. And then all of a sudden, you see the end of your playing career cresting the horizon, rushing towards you like a train you cannot evade.

37 Jeffri Chadiha, "Life after NFL a Challenge for Many," ESPN, ESPN Internet Ventures, May 31, 2012, https://www.espn.com/nfl/story/_/id/7983790/life-nfl-struggle-many-former-players.

38 Chadiha, "Life after NFL," ESPN.

Soon, the question that was naturally next burned in my mind: *What am I going to do?* Not wanting to wait until the final hour, I used my last semester at UMD to search for a job I could have upon graduation. I say *job* because that is truly what I was looking for, not a career. I hadn't thought through what my vocation truly was. I had no idea what the rest of my life held.

And if your daughter or son is not preparing for this transition now, neither will they.

Sadly, I have seen many athletes grapple with situations far worse than mine when they came to this monumental shift in their lives. If an athlete is not intentional about looking beyond a life playing sports, they can expect to struggle with this transition.

In an interview with *NCAA Champion Magazine*, assistant professor of kinesiology at the University of North Carolina at Greensboro Erin Reifsteck says,

A lot of the student-athletes I've worked with haven't really grappled with it until it's kind of right in their face and they're getting ready to graduate. The research suggests that proactive coping is really important. So, not waiting until after you're experiencing the transition to deal with it, but to have some pre-retirement planning.[39]

39 Rachel Stark, "When the Playing Days End: An NCAA Champion Feature," *NCAA Champion Magazine*, 2018, https://www.ncaa.org/static/champion/ when-the-playing-days-end/.

So how do we help prepare our kids for this difficult transition through what Reifsteck calls *proactive coping*? There are a few key things that can help set our children up for this transition well before they will ever have to think about *hanging 'em up*.

HELP THEM UNDERSTAND THE NUMBERS

It will serve our daughters and sons well to understand from an early age the statistics around sports and competing at the highest level. We definitely do not want to snatch our kids' dreams away before they have even had a chance to chase them, but it is important to help them understand how high and treacherous the mountain that they hope to climb actually is.

Like most mountains, the higher an athlete ascends, the less space there is at the top to stand. As your daughter or son climbs the various levels of their sport, the spots available will narrow, thus heightening the competition level. There is less space moving from pre-high school competition to high school, from high school to college, and so on.

And at the peak—in this case, professional athletics—there is only room for the most dedicated and talented athletes *who also have circumstances turn out in their favor*. That means *in addition to* working incredibly hard and being a gifted athlete, your child can have no career-derailing injuries, unfair coaches that hinder their chances beyond repair, or any other unavoidable circumstances that prevent this dream from materializing.

Statistically, it is very unlikely that our daughters and sons will be able to break into this exclusive group of professionals.

Take the NBA, for example. Doing some rough math, we find that there are less than 5,000 NBA players ... in the history of the league ... like, *ever*.

Let that sink in for a second.

That means if you brought together every player to ever be listed on an NBA roster (even just for one game) in the league's seventy-year history, you couldn't even fill some high school football stadiums.

And odds to play men's collegiate basketball aren't exactly favorable either. According to the NCAA, only 3.5% of male high school basketball players actually play in the NCAA. And only 1% of those players play on a Division I team.[40]

These sorts of numbers are consistent across all sports. That means, for most athletes, that our careers are ending far sooner than we wish them to. This can be a difficult reality for athletes to grapple with, especially if they do not fully consider the reality of the situation.

Again, this isn't about talking your children out of pursuing high-level athletics so much as it is about motivating them to work even harder if that is truly their goal. It will also help them see that playing professionally is not big enough to be their *only* dream, even if they do make it to the professional level.

---

40 "Men's Basketball: Probability of Competing beyond High School," NCAA.org, The Official Site of the NCAA, April 20, 2020, https://www.ncaa.org/about/resources/research/mens-basketball-probability-competing-beyond-high-school.

Here are some more numbers to consider. The average NBA career lasts four and a half years,[41] meaning most players are done with their career before they even turn twenty-seven years old. (I'll let you guess how many of those players *chose* retirement less than five years into their dream career.) Imagine chasing something your whole life and having it come to an end all before you even hit thirty. And, as we have already established, that's one of the best-case scenarios.

Therefore, it is helpful for our kids to see sports as a springboard to something far better. This means encouraging an even greater vision for their lives. Sports can be an amazing part of that vision, but it is more a means than it is an end.

HELP THEM UNDERSTAND SPORTS AS A MEANS

Former three-year player-captain of Duke basketball Sue Gordon says, "Know that the magic isn't in the game, the magic is in you. Everything that made you a success at your sport is what will make you a success in any endeavor if you call on it."[42]

This means a lot considering Gordon served as principal executive of national intelligence for the United States government. This is the picture we want to give our children: what life could be like *because* of sports and all it has taught them.

---

41 "Life after NBA Comes Sooner than Many Players Think," NBA.com/nuggets, July 21, 2015, https://www.nba.com/nuggets/features/junior_bridgeman_20100610.html#.

42 Prim Siripipat, "Moving on from Sports: A College Athlete's Greatest Challenge," ESPN, April 11, 2016, https://www.espn.com/espnw/voices/story/_/id/15182997/moving-sports-college-athlete-greatest-challenge.

And these are not conversations you have to wait to have. Help them to understand that whenever the day comes that their playing career is over, they will want to already have a vision for what comes next.

When they're at a young age, this looks like helping our daughters and sons diversify their interests outside of sports. Obviously their athletic journey will have to take a priority if they truly want to compete at a high level, but that doesn't mean it has to be the only thing in their lives.

Help them to see that joy in this life does not have to be related to their athletic journey. It is hugely beneficial to encourage our children to have hobbies and interests unrelated to sports. Maybe they play an instrument, love to write, take to learning a foreign language, have a passion for art, are fascinated with history or science or math. Whatever their interests, nurture those things from a young age.

As they get a little bit older—into middle school—have some conversations with your child and encourage them to dream. *Whenever you are done playing sports, what career do you think might interest you?* It is okay for them to not have an answer at this young age, but just by asking them the question, you prompt their mind to consider that this will one day become a reality.

When they are in high school, have some serious conversations about what majors they could imagine enjoying once they're in college. Again, they don't have to have it all figured out, but at least spark their thinking and have them research the various areas of study they get to choose from.

In college, ask them about their post-playing career, how they are feeling about it and what they are hoping for. Allow them space to be sad about the loss that they soon will face, but also encourage them to start the acceptance process earlier rather than later.

Encourage them to build their network all throughout their years in college. Remind them that the work world is not about *what you know* but *who you know*. Who are they building intentional relationships with now that will benefit them in the future? Have them build genuine and appropriate friendships with professors, faculty, university alumni, and university donors. In my experience, people associated with the university love to connect with athletes and help them out through references and connections. Obviously this is not about using others, but about allowing someone to help you in the same way you would help them, given the chance.

As they start the final year of their collegiate career, ask them about their plan after graduation.

How are you starting now to find career opportunities when you graduate? What are a few dream companies or organizations you are excited about? What entry-level opportunities do those companies and organizations have? Who do you know of with a connection? How are you reaching out now to start your own connection? When is the best time to apply? Have you consulted with your school's career center? What are your back-up opportunities you plan to pursue? Who else in your network are you reaching out to in order to learn about other opportunities?

These sorts of questions can be invaluable for our children as they consider their future beyond sports.

Remind them that they are more than ready and their history in sports has actually equipped them to succeed far beyond what they may expect.

There is a reason executives and human resources departments are drawn to former athletes—and their athletic history is something your daughter or son should make apparent on their resume. The transferable skills they have gained playing sports will serve them immensely when entering the workforce—not to mention benefitting the company or organization they end up with.

Leadership, perseverance, discipline, structure, teamwork, loyalty, hard work, excellence. All I had learned through my years of sports experience was already coming in handy less than a year into my journey into full-time work. What I did not know was how many options I had because of these skills.

A year after graduating college, I was working in a rather uninteresting field. One day I received a call from a buddy of mine. As this was prior to the advent of social media (and the internet, for that matter), I had little idea of what this friend was up to as of late. I was surprised to hear that he was working for the Washington Wizards, the NBA franchise in our nation's capital.

You can have a career in sports? I thought. This may seem obvious to you, but honestly the field hadn't crossed my mind as an option. Without hesitation, I applied with the Wizards and was able to land a job.

A dormant fire within me sparked! And I felt excited about life for the first time since finishing my playing career.

Because sports is such a gift to so many, there are a myriad of opportunities to work in the sports world. Those interested can work at league offices, for sports franchises, or with an athletic brand in management, sales, marketing, community relations, and the like. They can become a coach, trainer, work in the fitness industry or youth sports, and so on. The opportunities are plentiful.

And working in the sports world is a lot of fun! Take it from me. I've been in this industry for more than three decades, and I can honestly say it has been a blast. I get to attend games and watch some of the best athletes in the world, work with young people, and be around the sport I love all day long. I am passionate about getting up each morning because I am living the dream.

Though I do not *play* in the NBA, my dream was fulfilled in a way I never expected. Let's help our daughters and sons see this as a realistic option for them to pursue if they truly have a love for sports the way I do.

HELP THEM UNDERSTAND THE IMPORTANCE OF GIVING BACK

Tennis legend Arthur Ashe once said, "True heroism is remarkably sober, very undramatic. It is not the urge to surpass all others at whatever cost, but the urge to serve others at whatever cost."

This sort of service is another big part of fulfillment beyond sports for a former athlete. The selflessness learned through sports can transfer to other areas of their adult life when they are intentional about it. This means giving back with both time and resources to those who are in need.

As I have mentioned before, this is a habit you will want to instill in your kids from an early age, but I also encourage you to remind them of this during the pivotal transition from college to the workforce.

One of the frequent questions I ask athletes that are looking for a way to give back is, *do you have a cause?* What I mean is, do they have something important to them that allows them to actively practice putting others before themselves? Another helpful question to ask is, *where does your heart break for others?* Often this will have a link to something personal from your daughter's or son's own story.

For me, there are a few places where I intentionally give my time and my resources. When I was growing up, my family did not have much. As a result, I am intentional about helping out those who are hungry. I had a few caring adults that helped me when I was young, therefore I love supporting young people who are struggling and come from underprivileged areas. My mom played a special role in my life, so when I see other mothers going through something similar, my heart breaks and I am compelled to help. These are just a few examples.

Have intentional conversations with your children (and yourself) about the areas in which they would like to give back.

As they make the practice of giving back a habit, the sense of fulfillment and joy they will find will be unparalleled. It can build in us a sense of empathy (I can feel for others), a sense of reflection (I am not immune to these struggles), and a sense of gratitude (I have been given so much).

And as we think outside ourselves, we all can start to see that Jackie Robinson was right when he said, "A life is not important except in the impact it has on other lives."

A FINAL THOUGHT

I take solace in the fact that I have lived a full and amazing life— far richer than I ever could have imagined. God has used sports to bring about such good in my life and in the lives of my family.

Because of sports I have had a chance to see the world, have incredible experiences, and watch firsthand some of the greatest athletes on the planet. Though not perfect, I learned what it looks like to be a good person, employee, boss, spouse, and parent. The transferable skills of sports taught me how to walk a life well lived.

As we come to the end of this journey together, know that my hope is for your children to experience this sort of preparation for life through sports. That they would experience all the great things being an athlete can bring when we approach our craft with discipline, determination, and joy.

I also encourage you and your children to enjoy this process. If we always dream, we are never awake to enjoy the life that we have now. Live in the present and enjoy the moments you have together.

As the wise philosopher once said, "The great science to live happily is to live in the present."[43]

---

43 Pythagoras.

COACHES' APPENDIX

PARTNERING WITH PARENTS

"A good coach can change a game, a great coach can change a life." This incredible truth—immortalized in the words of the great John Wooden—serves as a coaching North Star. As a coach myself, I know how easy it is to lose sight of this truth and to get caught up in the demands, the stress, the frustration, the ego. But even when we are off track, the desire to be a coach that not only impacts a particular sport but *impacts lives* can guide us back to what makes coaching such a rewarding and important craft in the first place.

Though I wrote this book with parents in mind, there is so much here for us youth sport coaches to adapt and apply if we understand properly our role in this remarkable calling: *to partner with parents in educating and protecting young athletes as we prepare them for life in and beyond sports*. This means we must be willing coworkers with parents who want to use sports as a springboard in raising athletes who are also healthy and successful individuals.

When you approach the task of a coach with this as your highest goal, you will find the contents of this book hold powerful coaching truths that I have gleaned over my many years in the sports industry. That said, there are a few aspects of your role that I would love for you to consider more particularly, and I'll lay them out for you in this section.

IT STARTS WITH US

As coaches in youth sports, we must take seriously the call to "leave the game better than we found it."[44] Sometimes I am saddened at what we find in youth sports today. On any given weekend, we can find fields or gyms full of the joy of young people engaging in athletic competition—and on the same fields and in those same gyms are many adults doing their best to be less mature than the kids they are supporting or coaching. It does not surprise me that participation in youth sports seems to be declining in America and that players are switching teams more frequently than ever.

These issues are complex, and pursuing a *single* root cause will end fruitlessly. But it is not too much to say that if we want to see youth sports change for the better, it is going to start with us as coaches. In short, the way we coach matters. It matters to those we are leading and to the communities we are a part of.

Like all teams and organizations, culture can be most affected by those who are leading it. When someone opts to coach youth sports, they are agreeing to be a leader of young people. If we are to see the youth sports world change for the better, we must take this charge of leadership seriously, and lead with integrity and high character. In this, we model for the players entrusted to our care a way of living that will serve them well.

---

44 Original source unknown.

FOUNDATION OF RESPECT

If you have not already read through this book, I must tell you that respect is a major theme within it. I explore this theme in great length in chapter two; there I define *respect* as valuing someone or something with proper regard. For an athlete, this sort of respect should extend to themselves, others, and the sport they play.

Unsurprisingly, respect is not only foundational for those who want to be successful athletes, but also for those who want to be successful coaches. As a coach, I demand a lot of my players, and at times players are not going to like the way I do things. But I work really hard to respect those I coach, and to care first about their development as players and people. Thus I make it a point to coach fairly, not play favorites, and consider my players in all I do as a coach.

This means learning to communicate well and understand the way my players learn. I take my cue from coach Mike Krzyzewski who says, "A common mistake among those who work in sport is spending a disproportional amount of time on 'x's and o's' as compared to time spent learning about people." When I take the time to learn my players and learn how people tick, I become a better teacher, can make clear the expectations that I plan to hold my players to, and am able to lead my team in chasing after our shared and individual goals simultaneously.

It is also vital, then, that I avoid disrespectful and less developed forms of communication such as excessive shouting, cussing, belittlement, name-calling, and embarrassment tactics, as these do not treat our players with proper value. Plus, that's the old school way of coaching.

Respect also means that we model for and teach our players the right way to approach the game, and not in any way to try to shirk hard work or avoid operating with integrity. Remember that, as you are in a leadership position, you are at all times representing your community. This means demanding of your players that they show up prepared, ready to work hard, and bringing their best. We as coaches also have a responsibility to lead our players away from cheating, dirty play, and dishonest means of advancement. These dishonest approaches to sports only work against our goal of helping parents raise quality people.

The coach who purposely leads from a place of disrespect has no place in youth sports.

This sort of respect should also extend to an athlete's parents. This starts with the way we speak to them and their children. If we are disrespectful or noncommunicative in our interactions, we will reap difficulty in our connection with parents of players. I have seen far too many coaches get in shouting matches—or worse—with parents because of poor communication.

Not only so, but it is vital as well to show respect to both your players and their parents by being organized, being on time, ending practice when you say you will, and giving parents a good sense of the schedule and calendar.

Next, it is integral that we as coaches respect each parent with honest and up-front information about the time and financial commitment they are entering into; unfair fees and unhealthy time expectations show immense disrespect for families. Let us also approach parents with empathy for their unique situation and the willingness to work within reason to accommodate those in need. Furthermore, we have a responsibility to teach the ins and outs of our particular expression of youth sports to new families, helping them understand the values of our team and how the league we coach in works.

Pouring into parents this way is a huge part of coaching in the youth sports world and the importance of this sort of respect cannot be underestimated.

SETTING YOUR COACHING VALUES

Similar to families, I also recommend you take the time to think through the core values of the teams you are leading. Adapt— with your assistant coaches if applicable—the *Family Values Worksheet* at the end of chapter one to come up with your own team values. This will help ingrain in your mind the kind of coach you want to be and the kind of teams you want to be a part of. Consider the following questions:

- What do you want your team and your coaching to be known for?
- What sort of values will assist your players both on and off the field/court?
- When thinking about the goals you have for your team, what traits would serve them best?
- What is your coaching philosophy?
- What are your expectations of both players and parents?

Having core values as a coach also helps you to set expectations with players and parents before the season. This is what sets up a winning team culture. When it comes to team culture, though, you cannot just talk about it. You have to *be* about it. Model and repeat these values often. Praise players and parents when they embody these values well and respectfully hold to account those who miss the mark—even when it is you yourself. Practice your values with integrity. It can be tempting to play favorites or hold players to account unevenly—this is especially a temptation when faced with very talented athletes—but this will betray the trust of your team and will corrode team culture from the inside out.

This principled style of coaching includes holding parents accountable, showing them how stepping outside the team values impacts their own child and the rest of the team. If we have a parent that insists on speaking to the referees disrespectfully, it is important we have a conversation with them about the respect that is expected of them when their child is playing on the team.

As far as which values you should infuse into your team culture, that is certainly something for you to take your time and consider. When they come from your own convictions—and the convictions of those you are coaching alongside—there is a far greater chance these values will stick and be conveyed with authenticity.

That said, I offer many worthwhile values in this book for you to consider for your team. I hope that as you consider your role in helping parents leverage sports as a means of growth and advancement for their children, you will find and employ values that help to change the lives of your players forever.

ACKNOWLEDGEMENTS

This book has been brewing in my mind for about seven years. I feel strongly that it is my responsibility—considering all I have been blessed with throughout my own sports journey—to give back to all the parents who have kids in sports. Thank you for prioritizing your children and their dreams. I share with you my experience as an athlete, coach, sports business executive, and, most of all, a parent.

I also want to thank the team that helped me bring this book to life. Thank you, Drew Tilton of Asio Creative, for helping me bring this dream to fruition; Jessica Snell, for your quality editing; and Natalie Lauren Design, for the stellar design of this book.

Finally, a big thank you to my high school football coach, Mike Halley, for being a wonderful role model and showing me what it means to be a great coach and person. You taught me how to handle myself as an athlete on the field and a man of character in the world.